# Pattern and Voice

## An Anthology of Verse

Compiled by

John and Dorothy Colmer

**M**

First published 1981 by
THE MACMILLAN COMPANY OF AUSTRALIA PTY LTD
107 Moray Street, South Melbourne 3205
6 Clarke Street, Crows Nest 2065
Reprinted 1981, 1982, 1984 (twice), 1985, 1986, 1987

Associated companies
and representatives
throughout the world

National Library of Australia
cataloguing in publication data
Colmer, John, 1921 —
    Pattern and voice.

    Indexes
    ISBN 0 333 33705 0
    1. English Poetry. I. Colmer, Dorothy, II. Title.
821'.008

Set in Century by Graphicraft Typesetters, Hong Kong
Printed in Hong Kong

# Contents

## Enjoyment of Words                                                19

## Ballads                                                          39

## Songs                                                            53

## Sonnets

## Dramatic Verse

## Reflective Verse

## Myth, Prophecy and Vision

## The Poet's Eye

## Experimental                                               211

## Appendix: On Discussing Poetry                             217

# Preface

There are no poems by that good contemporary poet, Adrian Mitchell, in this anthology. That is because in one of his books he requests that none of his work should be used for examination purposes. Judith Wright is another poet who is very wary of the way poetry is taught and tested, but since she has not forbidden it, those two old favourites, 'Bullocky' and 'South of My Days', which are classics of the Australian scene, are offered here for the pleasure of a generation which may not yet have encountered them.

## Voice

It is easy to see why poets dislike examinations when one meets questions such as 'What is the poet really saying here?' Such questions assume that the poet has tried to say something but has not managed it very well and that the 'message' needs to be sorted out by the examinee, or that the poem is a puzzle to which the reader must provide a solution. Such a process by-passes the poem itself. A poem is a created object with a particular form either chosen from pre-existing patterns or invented for the occasion; it is made up of words and images in a particular sequence of time. Just as a small heap of broken glass is not the same as a graceful and elegant crystal vase, so the 'substance' or 'message' of a poem is no substitute for the poem itself, certainly not an improvement on it. In addition to shape, the sound of the poem matters, and so too do mood, tone, and the poet's chosen approach. These make up the personal voice of the poet, the things which make every poem different and every good poem memorable.

This is not to say that a slovenly disregard for meaning should be encouraged. The sensible reader looks at what the poet actually writes and what it means, but he or she must also be aware that poems are not simply statements or messages. Many different situations trigger off the writing of a poem. Sometimes it is a sense of one moment of feeling completely and fully alive. Such a poem is 'Their Faces Shone with Some Radiance' by Dylan Thomas. Other poems may make a joke, or reflect a sense of loss, or commemorate a friend, or voice a protest. Some may suggest very complex states of mind, as when D.J. Enright shows the curious sensations of 'The Sensitive Philanthropist' who is made uneasy and even repelled by mutilated beggars, yet sympathises with their lot to the extent of giving a limited amount of money. This attempt to put the substance of his poem into other words necessarily omits the sense of directly addressing the beggar, and yet that sense of direct confrontation is essential to the poem as a whole.

## Substance

Where the poem is one of social comment or protest there may be something akin to a 'message', but it is unlikely to be reducible to a single statement. Bruce Dawe's 'The Not-So-Good Earth', for instance, does not say 'suffering should not be reported on TV', nor does it say 'TV causes insensitivity to suffering'. What it does is to present a piece of action in which ordinary every-day people, not too unlike ourselves, are more concerned with focussing their television set than with the painful realities that the cameras show. Many readers find it a deeply disturbing poem, although it also has its comic aspect. This feeling of being disturbed, of being brought uneasily right into a recognisable situation, is the result of reading or hearing the whole. It cannot be aroused by presenting the substance of the poem in some other form of words.

At the furthest reach from poems of social comment are those written for the pure enjoyment of words and images, such as Masefield's 'Cargoes', bardic celebrations and glimpses of visionary worlds, which may be as different from each other as the Australian Aboriginal poem 'Dreamtime', Ted Hughes's black 'Crow' poems, or the rich artistry of Yeats's 'Sailing to Byzantium'. All of these need intelligent application to the meaning of the words, remembering that the words are combined to create forms in which sound, the sequence of images and the order of the design make up an indivisible whole. The only valid test of understanding a poem is the ability to read it aloud well. Unfortunately a very high proportion of students reach university level without ever having discovered the art of reading aloud.

## Form

Form is necessary to all poetry. Free verse is perhaps the hardest form of all to write really well. In free verse there is no regularly recurring rhythmic beat to shape the lines, no prescribed length of line, no rhyme, sometimes not even punctuation. How then does the poet structure the poem? He or she must work by ear and eye. The ear tests out the phrases into which the words group themselves; the eye must judge how to set out the poem on the page so that the reader can pick up the timing and speed of phrases and know when to pause. E.E. Cummings's 'Chanson Innocente' is a good example of such considered lay-out on the page.

Free verse is very commonly used in the twentieth century and many poets refuse to work in any other form. One even goes so far as to say that forcing a poem into a prearranged form is as bad as cutting off the claws of a living lobster to force it into the cooking-pot. But many poets look for a more obvious patterning than free verse provides. Some add rhymes or alliteration to free verse; some use repetitive phrase-patterns to form a kind of rhythm; some count syllables and produce, for example, a poem in which every line has exactly seven syllables.

By far the commonest alternatives to free verse are the traditional metrical forms. Many wood-carvers like to work with hard-grained wood, using the pre-existing grain and knots as part of their design, and sculptors may prefer resistant marble to malleable clay; just so many poets prefer to work with forms that impose limitations. Sonnets, ballads, villanelles, and limericks all have their appropriate metrical forms, but the examples in this book will show that these fixed patterns allow expression to a wide variety of voices. It should not be forgotten that regular metrical stanzas can be created by the individual artist for a particular purpose. Judith Wright is a particularly creative stanza-maker. Supporters of metrical forms point out that regular rhythm is part of nature. Our hearts beat, we breathe, we walk in rhythm; and many jobs of work, hauling ropes, chopping wood, digging, fall into rhythmic patterns.

## Modes

As well as choosing between metre and freer verse pattern, a poet may be influenced by another set of poetic forms which may be called modes. These relate to mood and occasion. Thus many poems are elegiac; they express a mood of lamentation or nostalgia. Yet within a single mode poets may choose many different forms of versification. David Campbell's 'The Boy' is a regular sonnet, Peter Skrzynecki's 'Elegy for Don McLaughlin' is free verse, and Howard Sergeant's 'The Inarticulate' is in rhymed verse with irregular metre. All three, however, are elegies. Other modes are the meditative or reflective, which may sometimes take a comic turn. Then there are odes, which are always written in rather formal and ceremonial language. In ancient Greek times, odes were chanted aloud by a chorus wheeling in the movement and countermovement of a slow dance. In the dramatic mode, a character directly addresses another person or speaks his thoughts aloud without restraint and so, often, gives away more of himself than he realises.

Several sections, particularly 'The Poet's Eye', show how poets will choose or create whatever form suits both their temperament and their subject. Through whatever pattern he adopts or creates, the poet speaks with an individual voice.

## Memory

All good poems are memorable, and worth memorising. If you like a poem, try reading it over and over again, aloud if possible, until you have it by heart. Books may be lost or handed on, but memory stays, and a well-stocked memory is a priceless treasure that costs nothing at all.

# Satire and Social Comment

One function of the poet, suggests Coleridge, is to lift 'the film of familiarity' from life. He is likely therefore to make us more critical of things that habit has led society to accept. The kind of poetry that seeks to correct human follies and social abuses by holding them up to ridicule is verse satire. The great period for this form was the eighteenth century, when Pope perfected the heroic couplet as a medium for polished witty satire. In his satirical elegy on the famous Duke of Marlborough, another eighteenth-century poet, Jonathan Swift, uses the occasion of the famous general's death to hold him up to scorn and ridicule in witty ironic octosyllabic couplets. Such poems on famous individuals do not date, because great satiric portraits in verse acquire a representative quality so that they can be seen to apply to similar types in all ages.

Even though few poets write formal verse satires in couplets today, many comment satirically on personal follies and social abuses. The range of subjects for social comment is enormously wide, as the poems in this section reveal. They extend from mass pollution of Lake Erie in Andrew Taylor's poem to the ridicule of whole cities, as in Chris Wallace Crabbe's 'Melbourne' and a whole country in Wynford Vaughan-Thomas's 'Farewell to New Zealand', described as 'Super-suburbia of the Southern Seas'.

A common feature of many of the poems in this section is their use of wit and humour. Where politicians solemnly promise to improve society and often bore us to death with empty platitudes, the social poet entertains us while making us think more deeply about what is wrong with society. The Australian poet Peter Porter shows amusing ingenuity in adapting the pattern of the consumer questionnaire used by advertisers to express his sardonic rejection of modern life. An earlier English poet, Arthur Hugh Clough, ingeniously adapts the Biblical ten commandments to suit the actual behaviour of his time, producing among others the memorable and often quoted couplet:

> Thou shalt not kill; but needst not strive
> Officiously to keep alive.

In a pointed and witty fashion these lines identify a hypocritical stand that is prevalent in government and public affairs. The kind of poem that condenses its wit into very few lines is the epigram. An example is Coleridge's 'On a Bad Singer':

> Swans sing before they die: 't were no bad thing
> Did certain persons die before they sing.

Some subjects are so heartrending they seem to rule out humour. There are therefore a number of poems in this section that dispense with the satirist's main weapons of wit and humour and make their point through other means. Kevin Gilbert casts his poem about the position of aborigines in Australia in the form of a direct address to the white reader by an indignant aboriginal voice:

> What is it you want
> Whiteman?

In her 'Fire Sermon', Judith Wright uses a variety of devices to make us aware of the gap between official statements and the actual suffering of the Asian people during war. Like many poets represented in this section, she broods on the vividness but remoteness of poverty and suffering in the Television Age. Of the suffering child she sees on her screen she says:

> I can't put out a hand to touch her,
> that shadow printed on glass.

People living affluent lives find it easy to look at poverty and war from the comfortable distance of their armchairs. Two poems in this section illustrate the poet's power to shock us into facing the harsh reality we prefer to ignore. In his satiric poem 'The Not-so-Good Earth', Bruce Dawe builds up an ironic contrast between the appalling suffering pictured on the TV screen and the uncaring ordinariness of the family group watching. The free verse form is especially apt for capturing the ordinary voice of the person describing the family scene. And the descriptive details combine to make the point that far-off hardships have been transformed into just another 'spectacle' on TV. By contrast, the oriental scene is less dramatic in D.J. Enright's 'The Sensitive Philanthropist'. The voice that speaks to us in this poem is of the man who is prepared to give money to the poor and suffering, provided they do not disturb his comfortable way of life.

> If I give you money
> Will you agree
> To hide your stump away
> Where I can't see it?

The satirist and social poet remind us of all those aspects of life that we find it comfortable to ignore and hope will just go away.

## The Men Who Made Australia
(*Written on the Occasion of the Royal Visit to Australia, 1901*)

There'll be royal times in Sydney for the Cuff and Collar Push,
  There'll be lots of dreary drivel and clap-trap
From the men who own Australia, but who never knew the Bush,
  And who could not point their runs out on the map.
Oh, the daily Press will grovel as it never did before,
  There'll be many flags of welcome in the air,
And the Civil Service poet, he shall write odes by the score—
  But the men who made the land will not be there.

You shall meet the awful Lady of the latest Birthday Knight—
  (She is trying to be English, don't-cher-know?)
You shall hear the empty mouthing of the champion blatherskite,
  You shall hear the boss of local drapers blow.
There's 'majahs' from the counter, tailors' dummies from the fleet,
  And to represent Australia here today,
There's the toady with his card-case and his cab in Downing Street;
  But the men who made Australia—where are they?

Call across the blazing sand wastes of the Never-Never Land!
  There are some who will not answer yet awhile,
Some whose bones rot in the mulga or lie bleaching on the sand,
  Died of thirst to win the land another mile.
Thrown from horses, ripped by cattle, lost on deserts: and the weak,
  Mad through loneliness or drink (no matter which),
Drowned in floods or dead of fever by the sluggish slimy creek—
  These are men who died to make the Wool-Kings rich.

There are carriages in waiting for the swells from over-sea,
  There are banquets in the latest London style,
While the men who made Australia live on damper, junk and tea—
  But the quiet voices whisper, 'Wait a while!'
For the sons of all Australia, they were born to conquer fate—
  And, where charity and friendship are sincere,
Where a sinner is a brother and a stranger is a mate,
  There the future of a nation's written clear.

Aye, the cities claim the triumphs of a land they do not know,
  But all empty is the day they celebrate!
For the men who made Australia federated long ago,
  And the men to rule Australia—they can wait.
Though the bed may be the rough bunk or the gum leaves or the sand,
  And the roof for half the year may be the sky—
There are men among the Bushmen who were born to save the land!
  And they'll take their places sternly by-and-by.

HENRY LAWSON

## Aboriginal Query

What is it you want
Whiteman?
What do you need from me?
You have taken my life
My culture
My dreams
You have leached the substance
Of love from my being
You have leached the substance
Of race from my loins
Why do you persist?
Is it because you are a child
Whose callous inquisitiveness probes
As a finger questing
To wreck a cocoon
To find the chrysalis inside
To find
To explore
To break open
To learn anew
That nothing new is learned
And like a child
With all a child's brutality
Throw the broken chrysalis to the ground
Then run unthinking
To pull asunder the next
What do you seek?
Why do you destroy me
Whiteman?
Why do you destroy that
Which you cannot hope to understand . . .

KEVIN   GILBERT

## Melbourne

Not on the ocean, on a muted bay
Where the broad rays drift slowly over mud
And flathead loll on sand, a city bloats
Between the plains of water and of loam.
If surf beats, it is faint and far away;
If slogans blow around, we stay at home.

And, like the bay, our blood flows easily,
Not warm, not cold (in all things moderate),
Following our familiar tides. Elsewhere

Victims are bleeding, sun is beating down
On patriot, guerrilla, refugee.
We see the newsreels when we dine in town.

Ideas are grown in other gardens while
This chocolate soil throws up its harvest of
Imported and deciduous platitudes,
None of them flowering boldly or for long;
And we, the gardeners, securely smile
Humming a bar or two of rusty song.

Old tunes are good enough if sing we must;
Old images, re-vamped *ad nauseam,*
Will sate the burgher's eye and keep him quiet
As the great wheels run on, and should he seek
Variety, there's wind, there's heat, there's frost
To feed his conversation all the week.

Highway by highway the remorseless cars
Strangle the city, put it out of pain,
Its limbs still kicking feebly on the hills.
Nobody cares. The artists sail at dawn
For brisker ports, or rot in public bars.
Though much has died here, little has been born.

CHRIS   WALLACE-CRABBE

## Farewell to New Zealand

Super-suburbia of the Southern Seas,
Nature's—and Reason's—true Antipodes,
Hail, dauntless pioneers, intrepid souls,
Who cleared the Bush—to make a lawn for bowls,
And smashed the noble Maori to ensure
The second-rate were socially secure!
Saved by the Wowsers from the Devil's Tricks,
Your shops, your pubs, your minds all close at six.
Your battle-cry's a deep, contented snore,
You voted Labour, then you worked no more.
The Wharfies' Heaven, the gourmet's Purgat'ry:
Ice-cream on mutton, swilled around in tea!

A Maori fisherman, the legends say,
Dredged up New Zealand in a single day.
I've seen the catch, and here's my parting crack—
It's under-sized; for God's sake throw it back!

WYNFORD   VAUGHAN-THOMAS

## The Not-So-Good Earth

For a while there we had 25-inch Chinese peasant families
famishing in comfort on the 25-inch screen
and even Uncle Billy whose eyesight's going fast
by hunching up real close to the convex glass
could just about make them out—the riot scene
in the capital city for example
he saw that better than anything, using the contrast knob
to bring them up dark—all those screaming faces
and bodies going under the horses' hooves—he did a terrific job
on that bit, not so successful though
on the quieter parts where they're just starving away
digging for roots in the not-so-good earth
cooking up a mess of old clay
and coming out with all those Confucian analects
to everybody's considerable satisfaction
(if I remember rightly Grandmother dies
with naturally a suspenseful break in the action
for a full symphony orchestra plug for Craven A
neat as a whistle probably damn glad
to be quit of the whole gang with their marvellous patience.)
We never did find out how it finished up . . . Dad
at this stage tripped over the main lead in the dark
hauling the whole set down smack on its inscrutable face,
wiping out in a blue flash and curlicue of smoke
600 million Chinese without a trace . . .

BRUCE   DAWE

## Fire Sermon

'Sinister powers,' the ambassador said, 'are moving
into our ricefields. We are a little people
and all we want is to live.'

But a chemical rain descending
has blackened the fields, and
we ate the buffalo because we were starving.

'Sinister powers,' he said;
and I look at the newsreel child
crying, crying quite silently, here in my house.

I can't put out a hand to touch her,
that shadow printed on glass.
And if I could? I look at my hand.

This hand, this sinister power
and this one here on the right side
have blackened your ricefields,
my child, and killed your mother.

In the temple the great gold Buddha
smiles inward with half-closed eyes.
All is Maya, the dance, the veil,
Shiva's violent dream.

Let me out of this dream, I cry.
I belong to a simple people
and all we want is to live.

'It is not right that we slay our kinsmen,'
Arjuna cried. And the answer?
'What is action, what is inaction?
By me alone are they doomed and slain.'

A hard answer
for those who are doomed and slain.

'All is fire,' said the Buddha, 'all—
sight, sense, all forms.
They burn with the fires of lust,
anger, illusion.

'Wherefore the wise man . . .'
'Be a lamp to yourself. Be an island.'

Let me out of this dream, I cry,
but the great gold Buddha
smiles in the temple
under a napalm rain.

JUDITH WRIGHT

## Epitaph on a Tyrant

Perfection, of a kind, was what he was after,
And the poetry he invented was easy to understand;
He knew human folly like the back of his hand,
And was greatly interested in armies and fleets;
When he laughed, respectable senators burst with laughter,
And when he cried the little children died in the streets.

W.H. AUDEN

## The Sensitive Philanthropist

If I give you money,
Give you baksheesh,
Will you stay away
Until next week?

Since money talks
We don't need to,
Neither you to me
Nor me to you.

If I give you money
Will you make sure
That the others keep away,
Without me giving more?

Will you promise
To put to flight
All your legless colleagues
By day and by night?

If I give you money
Will you agree
To hide your stump away,
Where I can't see?

Will you state in writing
That it was done on purpose
And doesn't really hurt,
The arms, the legs, the nose?

Can't I send a cheque
Regular each week
By registered letter,
So we need never meet?

D.J. ENRIGHT

## Always a Suspect

I get up in the morning
and dress up like a gentleman—
A white shirt a tie and a suit

I walk into the street
to be met by a man
who tells me to 'produce'.

I show him
the document of my existence
to be scrutinized and given the nod.

Then I enter the foyer of a building
to have my way barred by a commissionaire.
'What do you want?'

I trudge the city pavements
side by side with 'madam'
who shifts her handbag
from my side to the other,
and looks at me with eyes that say
'Ha! Ha! I know who you are;
beneath those fine clothes
ticks the heart of a thief.'

OSWALD   MBUYISENI   MTSHALI

## Holy Thursday

Is this a holy thing to see
In a rich and fruitful land,
Babes reduced to misery.
Fed with cold and usurous hand?

Is that trembling cry a song?
Can it be a song of joy?
And so many children poor?
It is a land of poverty!

And their sun does never shine,
And their fields are bleak and bare,
And their ways are filled with thorns:
It is eternal winter there.

For where-e'er the sun does shine,
And where-e'er the rain does fall,
Babe can never hunger there,
Nor poverty the mind appall.

WILLIAM   BLAKE

**A Satirical Elegy on the Death of a
Late Famous General, 1722**

His Grace! impossible! what dead!
Of old age too, and in his bed!
And could that Mighty Warrior fall?
And so inglorious, after all!
Well, since he's gone, no matter how,
The last loud trump must wake him now:
And, trust me, as the noise grows stronger,
He'd wish to sleep a little longer.
And could he be indeed so old
As by the news-papers we're told?
Threescore, I think, is pretty high;
'Twas time in conscience he should die.
This world he cumbered long enough;
He burnt his candle to the snuff;
And that's the reason, some folks think,
He left behind so great a stink.

Behold his funeral appears,
Nor widow's sighs, nor orphan's tears,
Wont at such times each heart to pierce,
Attend the progress of his hearse.
But what of that, his friends may say,
He had those honors in his day.
True to his profit and his pride,
He made them weep before he died.

Come hither, all ye empty things,
Ye bubbles raised by breath of Kings;
Who float upon the tide of state,
Come hither, and behold your fate.
Let pride be taught by this rebuke,
How very mean a thing's a Duke;
From all his ill-got honors flung,
Turned to that dirt from whence he sprung.

JONATHAN  SWIFT


**Of Common Devotion**

Our God and soldiers we alike adore,
Ev'n at the brink of danger; not before:
After deliverance, both alike requited,
Our God's forgotten, and our soldiers slighted.

FRANCIS  QUARLES

## Epitaph for the Unknown Soldier

To save your world, you asked this man to die:
Would this man, could he see you now, ask why?

W.H. AUDEN

## Sporus

   Yet let me flap this bug with gilded wings,
This painted child of dirt, that stinks and stings;
Whose buzz the witty and the fair annoys,
Yet wit ne'er tastes, and beauty ne'er enjoys:
So well-bred spaniels civilly delight
In mumbling of the game they dare not bite.
Eternal smiles his emptiness betray,
As shallow streams run dimpling all the way.
Whether in florid impotence he speaks,
And, as the prompter breathes, the puppet squeaks;
Or at the ear of Eve, familiar toad!
Half froth, half venom, spits himself abroad,
In puns, or politics, or tales, or lies,
Or spite, or smut, or rhymes, or blasphemies.
His wit all see-saw, between that and this,
Now high, now low, now master up, now miss,
And he himself one vile antithesis.
Amphibious thing! that acting either part,
The trifling head, or the corrupted heart;
Fop at the toilet, flatterer at the board,
Now trips a lady, and now struts a lord.
Eve's tempter thus the Rabbins have express'd,
A cherub's face, a reptile all the rest.
Beauty that shocks you, parts that none will trust,
Wit that can creep, and pride that licks the dust.

ALEXANDER POPE

## My Own Epitaph

Life is a jest, and all things show it.
I thought so once; but now I know it.

JOHN GAY

## Impromptu on Charles II

God bless our good and gracious King,
    Whose promise none relies on;
Who never said a foolish thing,
    Nor ever did a wise one.

ROCHESTER

## On a Bad Singer

Swans sing before they die:'t were no bad thing
Did certain persons die before they sing.

S.T. COLERIDGE

## The Latest Decalogue

Thou shalt have one God only, who
Would be at the expense of two?
No graven images may be
Worshipped, except the currency:
Swear not at all, for for thy curse
Thine enemy is none the worse:
At church on Sunday to attend
Will serve to keep the world thy friend:
Honour thy parents; that is, all
From whom advancement may befall:
Thou shalt not kill; but needst not strive
Officiously to keep alive:
Do not adultery commit;
Advantage rarely comes of it:
Thou shalt not steal; an empty feat,
When it's so lucrative to cheat:
Bear not false witness; let the lie
Have time on its own wings to fly:
Thou shalt not covet; but tradition
Approves all forms of competition.
The sum of all is, thou shalt love,
If any body, God above:
At any rate shall never labour
*More* than thyself to love thy neighbour.

ARTHUR   HUGH   CLOUGH

## Ethics for Everyman

Throwing a bomb is bad,
Dropping a bomb is good;
Terror, no need to add,
Depends on who's wearing the hood.

Kangaroo courts are wrong,
Specialist courts are right;
Discipline by the strong
Is fair if your collar is white.

Company output 'soars',
Wages, of course, 'explode';
Profits deserve applause,
Pay-claims, the criminal code.

Daily the Church declares
Betting-shops are a curse;
Gambling with stocks and shares
Enlarges the national purse.

Workers are absentees,
Businessmen relax,
Different as chalk and cheese;
   Social morality
   Has a duality —
One for each side of the tracks.

ROGER   WODDIS

## A Consumer's Report

The name of the product I tested is *Life*,
I have completed the form you sent me
and understand that my answers are confidential.
I had it as a gift,
I didn't feel much while using it,
in fact I think I'd have liked to be more excited.
It seemed gentle on the hands
but left an embarrassing deposit behind.
It was not economical
and I have used much more than I thought
(I suppose I have about half left
But it's difficult to tell) —
although the instructions are fairly large
there are so many of them
I don't know which to follow, especially
as they seem to contradict each other.
I'm not sure such a thing
should be put in the way of children —

It's difficult to think of a purpose
for it. One of my friends says
it's just to keep its maker in a job.
Also the price is much too high.
Things are piling up so fast,
after all, the world got by
for a thousand million years
without this, do we need it now?
(Incidentally, please ask your man
to stop calling me 'the respondent',
I don't like the sound of it.)
There seems to be a lot of different labels,
sizes and colours should be uniform,
the shape is awkward, it's waterproof
but not heat resistant, it doesn't keep
yet it's very difficult to get rid of:
whenever they make it cheaper they seem
to put less in—if you say you don't
want it, then it's delivered anyway.
I'd agree it's a popular product,
it's got into the language; people
even say they're on the side of it.
Personally I think it's overdone,
a small thing people are ready
to behave badly about. I think
we should take it for granted. If its
experts are called philosophers or market
researchers or historians, we shouldn't
care. We are the consumers and the last
law makers. So finally, I'd buy it.
But the question of a 'best buy'
I'd like to leave until I get
the competitive product you said you'd send.

PETER PORTER


## The Ice Fishermen, Lake Erie

Beside the steel plant
washed by sulphurous smoke
no sea wings
no clatter of beaks nor the sharp
antagonism of cries
no soughing of pines not even
the scribble and rage of ti-tree across cliffs
no scramble of dunes
no suck and hiss on the sand
no clink of shells
no shells
no sand

only the orange smoke spreading from stacks
only the shadows hurled across ice
the black forest of the steel plant
the cindered roads the wiry spike-riddle fence
the buffered ends
of the steel company railroad
the channel for freighters
the long-legged
meandering stride of the skyway humped over docks
slumped into swamps

the evening orange as the late light
blazes through smoke and steam from the steel plant
wings of smoke swoop darkly and glide off
somewhere out on the lake
the ghost of a breeze invokes the ghost of a flurry

as though they were skaters
as though they were fixed in nightmare on the ice
as though the music had stopped and each
bent in a miserly gesture towards hell
as though in a picnic on the ice

they had taken root
like the steel plant
on the ice on the dead lake they are

of all things they are fishing
fishing for fish
or the mercury trapped in the flesh
in the glands of the few poor
whatever lampreys could live there in the stench
and run-off from the steel plant
would they eat what they catch?

do they catch fish at all?

it being Sunday maybe this is really
an aspiration to hope
hope that beneath the ice something's thrashing and hungry
butting toward the sky just as they crouch
hunched over dark
hope that in the shadow of the steel plant
the hunger trapping them could be dragged up
into that air out of that lake

hope that they'll meet themselves there face to face
one drowning in air
feeding those huddled bodies that confront
that dying in air

ANDREW  TAYLOR

## Suburb with Television

Here we see (now quietly please)
our families relaxing
water-green as elvers
radiation gradually making clear
the shadow of their skeletons
within that paler shadow of the flesh.

Ah but really you should come in daytime
to catch the children
running up
to clutch their screen for comfort
*Mummy — Dad —*

RODNEY HALL

## Tree in the City

In the city branches are a small span
but still boys break at the brittle parts
before school, reaching above asphalt,
or they climb up as a convenient excuse
to pretend adventure in the old limbs
and they write their knees with necessary scratches
and their torn shirts feel the foreign soot
in corroded bark.

The Council has the power to trample on it
with a girl's finger lightly at a typewriter,
or it may even now be withering in secret, quietly.
Or the rough-chinned youths might fall upon it tonight
in the hours after no school remembered
because of the feel of a blade in their good hands
or something about it being there, living, and them
to accomplish nothing.

But today it is fact in a green accent
it is a live tree in this city
with its exuberances of new leaves
for all children to tear at and to fondle
to learn the feel of moistness still on them
to tell the truest way of year from.
It is a place to eat their lunches under
in shade, greedily.

THOMAS SHAPCOTT

## Near the School for Handicapped Children

His hat is rammed on
his shirt jerks at his body
his feet cannot hold in
      the sway    he cannot keep
                              still.
When I see his face it is freckled
to remind me of nephews
his limbs remind me of how straight
is my own spine and that I take my fingers
for granted.
He is waiting for the green light.
              my fingers clench
        I am hurt by my wholeness
        I cannot take my eyes from him
        I fear my daughter may be watching
He has been dressed carefully
      I'm here I'm here I'm here
his whole struggle rasps me like a whisper

and when the lights do change
      he skips across the road he
         skips he skips he dances and skips
            leaving us all behind like a skimming tamborine
            brittle with music.

                              THOMAS   SHAPCOTT

# Enjoyment of Words

Three of the qualities that distinguish human beings from other animals are their ability to use words, their skill at creating objects, and their love of amusing each other. These three qualities come together in games with words. Some of our earliest known poems are riddles, puzzles, and puns; and poets through the ages have continued the habit of getting and giving enjoyment from clever manipulation of words.

'The Yarn of the *Nancy Bell*' is a riddle: how could one man be:

> . . . a cook and a captain bold
> And the mate of the *Nancy* brig,
>   And a bo'sun tight, and a midshipmite,
> And the crew of the captain's gig.

Thomas Hood's 'Faithless Sally Brown' contains a series of absurd double meanings, the writer of 'Smiling Villain' invents new grammatical forms, and two Australian poets, C.J. Dennis and A.D. Hope have fun with place-names.

> O, there's little to be hoped from Grabben Gullen
> And Tumbulgum shrinks and shudders at its fate;
> Folks at Wantabadgery and Cullen Bullen
> Have Buckley's chance of reaching Heaven's gate.

In 'Cargoes', John Masefield savours words like a wine-taster, rolling them on his tongue. First he tries the exotic cargo of the ancient quinquireme, a ship rowed by five banks of oars. Next he tries the stately Spanish galleon laden with treasures and spice. All the treasures have long names containing sounds (M,N,S,Z) on which the voice can linger lovingly:

> . . . diamonds
> Emeralds, amethyst,
> Topazes, and cinnamon, and gold moidores.

Last comes the anticlimax of a dirty little steamship full of goods with jerky monosyllabic names such as 'pig-lead' and 'cheap tin trays'.

Alaric Watts exercises his ingenuity by writing a poem in which every word of the first line begins with A, the second with B and so on through the alphabet with the exception of J. Andrew Taylor uses a similar pattern but allows himself some free words and has more concern for sound than the actual letter. His X line is 'expire about him exhausted, exasperated, *in extremis*', while Watts has the initial letter X but the sound of Z in 'Xerxes, Ximenes, Xanthus, Xavier'.

'The Tale of Lord Lovell' is a parody, the imitation of a serious form for comic effect. Here the ballad style and old-fashioned language thinly disguise a very modern episode. Another parodic poem is D.J. Enright's 'An Ew Erra', which imitates typographical errors to suggest several things at the same time. It is a parody of poems in which different sizes of type are used and words spaced out or closed up to give unusual effects. It also contains many puns and double meanings. For example:

> The trypewiter is cretin
> A revultion in peotry.

This suggests not only a typewriter creating a revolution in poetry but also a cretin (idiot) writing tripe and causing a revulsion from poetry. The poem also contains echoes of traditional writers, of Hamlet's 'To be or not to be' soliloquy, of Blake's 'The Tiger', and of a speech in Marlowe's *Dr Faustus* — 'Why, this is Hell, nor am I out of it'.

There are some forms which it is impossible to parody because they are never serious. The limerick is one. The straight report of a small news item, for instance, might say: 'An unconfirmed report from Bihar states that an elderly man found dead by the roadside was at first thought to be the victim of a car-accident, but subsequent examination of his head revealed the presence of a small meteorite which had struck and killed him.' When this is recast in the form of a limerick, we have:

> An elderly man of Bihar
> Was killed, it appeared, by a car;
>     But they looked in his head
>     And discovered, instead,
> He'd been struck by a small falling star.

Nobody would ever take that seriously because the limerick pattern has become firmly associated with absurdity (and often with obscenity). Edward Lear was one of the first to popularise the form, but his limericks may sound odd to modern ears because he often uses the same word to end the first and last lines. Lear is justly famous for his nonsense songs, such as 'The Jumblies', in which inventive language is raised to a high level of creativity.

The Clerihew, invented by Edmund Clerihew Bentley, is another invariably absurd verse form. The epitaph on the other hand is usually quite solemn, a record of a dead person's virtues suitable for carving on a tombstone, but a surprising number of comic epitaphs exist as proof that men can make fun even of death.

### How to Spend New Year's Eve Alone

Andrew ambles along awkward and all anyhow
bemused by butterflies but bothered by Beate,
conjuring contemporary cadences and catchcries
designed to dull or diminish distance and despair.
Eventually everything emerges—
fascinatingly fateful for effeminate ephebes
guided generally by good grace and generosity.

Hardly hateful, but highlighting the hiatus
in their intense but international involvement,
genuinely dejecting Jeremiads and jaundicing
calamities and catastrophies collapse on him Karate-like?
like limbs of elms? like lugubrious
mumblings of monsters muttering malignant
nonsense, numbness, Nemesis? — No!
No! No! No!
Only oblivion!
Perhaps
quite quintessential qualities, quirky and quixotic
ramified in remote reaches, rarely researched
and seldom scrutinised
teach him to treasure topics technology
unthinkingly underestimates?
Valiant volition — but vain!

Wizardry, world-wobbling wonders, will-power, the works
expire about him exhausted, exasperated, *in extremis*,
yielding, yes yeastily yielding their yondermost yen,
the enzyme zero, or the Z of Zen.

ANDREW  TAYLOR

### An Austrian Army

An Austrian army awfully array'd,
Boldly by battery besieged Belgrade.
Cossack commanders cannonading come
Dealing destruction's devastating doom:
Every endeavour engineers essay,
For fame, for fortune fighting-furious fray!
Generals 'gainst generals grapple, gracious God!
How Heaven honours heroic hardihood!
Infuriate—indiscriminate in ill—
Kinsmen kill kindred—kindred kinsmen kill:
Labour low levels loftiest, longest lines,
Men march 'mid mounds, 'mid moles, 'mid murd'rous
    mines:
Now noisy noxious numbers notice nought
Of outward obstacles, opposing ought—
Poor patriots—partly purchased—partly press'd
Quite quaking, quickly 'Quarter! quarter!' quest:
Reason returns, religious right redounds,
Suwarrow stops such sanguinary sounds.
Truce to thee, Turkey, triumph to thy train,
Unwise, unjust, unmerciful Ukraine!
Vanish, vain victory! Vanish, victory vain!
Why wish we warfare? Wherefore welcome were
Xerxes, Ximenes, Xanthus, Xavier?
Yield, yield, ye youths, ye yeomen, yield your yell:
Zeno's, Zimmermann's, Zoroaster's zeal,
Again attract; arts against arms appeal!

ALARIC  A.  WATTS

### Faithless Sally Brown

Young Ben he was a nice young man,
    A carpenter by trade;
And he fell in love with Sally Brown,
    That was a lady's maid.

But as they fetched a walk one day,
    They met a press-gang crew;
And Sally she did faint away,
    Whilst Ben he was brought to.

The Boatswain swore with wicked words,
    Enough to shock a saint,
That though she did seem in a fit,
    'Twas nothing but a feint.

'Come, girl,' said he, 'hold up your head,
    He'll be as good as me;
For when your swain is in our boat,
    A boatswain he will be.'

So when they'd made their game of her,
    And taken off her elf,
She roused, and found she only was
    A coming to herself.

'And is he gone, and is he gone?'
    She cried, and wept outright:
'Then I will to the water side,
    And see him out of sight.'

A waterman came up to her,
    'Now, young woman,' said he,
'If you weep on so, you will make
    Eye-water in the sea.'

'Alas! they've taken my beau Ben,
    To sail with old Benbow;'
And her woe began to run afresh,
    As if she'd said, Gee woe!

Says he, 'They've only taken him
    To the Tender-ship, you see;'
'The Tender-ship,' cried Sally Brown,
    'What a hard-ship that must be!

'Oh! would I were a mermaid now,
    For then I'd follow him;
But Oh!—I'm not a fish-woman,
    And so I cannot swim.

'Alas! I was not born beneath
    The virgin and the scales,
So I must curse my cruel stars,
    And walk about in Wales.'

Now Ben had sailed to many a place
    That's underneath the world;
But in two years the ship came home,
    And all her sails were furled.

But when he called on Sally Brown,
    To see how she got on,
He found she'd got another Ben,
    Whose Christian-name was John.

'Oh, Sally Brown, oh, Sally Brown,
    How could you serve me so,
I've met with many a breeze before,
    But never such a blow!'

Then reading on his 'bacco box,
    He heaved a heavy sigh,
And then began to eye his pipe,
    And then to pipe his eye.

And then he tried to sing 'All's Well,'
    But could not, though he tried;
His head was turn'd, and so he chewed
    His pigtail till he died.

His death, which happened in his berth,
    At forty-odd befell:
They went and told the sexton, and
    The sexton tolled the bell.

                                THOMAS  HOOD


## The Yarn of the *Nancy Bell*

'Twas on the shores that round our coast
    From Deal to Ramsgate span,
That I found alone on a piece of stone
    An elderly naval man.

His hair was weedy, his beard was long,
    And weedy and long was he,
And I heard this wight on shore recite,
    In a singular minor key:

'Oh, I am a cook and a captain bold,
    And the mate of the *Nancy* brig,
And a bo'sun tight, and a midshipmite,
    And the crew of the captain's gig.'

And he shook his fists and he tore his hair,
    Till I really felt afraid,
For I couldn't help thinking the man had been drinking,
    And so I simply said:

'Oh, elderly man, it's little I know
    Of the duties of men of the sea,
But I'll eat my hand if I understand
    How you can possibly be

'At once a cook, and a captain bold,
     And the mate of the *Nancy* brig,
And a bo'sun tight, and a midshipmite,
     And the crew of the captain's gig.'

Then he gave a hitch to his trousers, which
     Is a trick all seamen larn,
And having got rid of a thumping quid,
     He spun this painful yarn:

''Twas in the good ship *Nancy Bell*
     That we sailed to the Indian sea,
And there on a reef we come to grief,
     Which has often occurred to me.

'And pretty nigh all o' the crew was drowned
     (There was seventy-seven o' soul),
And only ten of the *Nancy's* men
     Said "Here!" to the muster-roll.

'There was me and the cook and the captain bold,
     And the mate of the *Nancy* brig,
And the bo'sun tight, and a midshipmite,
     And the crew of the captain's gig.

'For a month we'd neither wittles nor drink,
     Till a-hungry we did feel,
So we drawed a lot, and accordin' shot
     The captain for our meal.

'The next lot fell to the *Nancy's* mate,
     And a delicate dish he made;
Then our appetite with the midshipmite
     We seven survivors stayed.

'And then we murdered the bo'sun tight,
     And he much resembled pig;
Then we wittled free, did the cook and me,
     On the crew of the captain's gig.

'Then only the cook and me was left,
     And the delicate question, "Which
Of us two goes to the kettle?" arose
     And we argued it out as sich.

'For I loved that cook as a brother, I did.
     And the cook he worshipped me;
But we'd both be blowed if we'd either be stowed
     In the other chap's hold, you see.

' "I'll be eat if you dines off me," says Tom,
    "Yes, that," says I, "you'll be,"—
"I'm boiled if I die, my friend," quoth I,
    And "Exactly so," quoth he.

'Says he, "Dear James, to murder me
    Were a foolish thing to do,
For don't you see that you can't cook *me*,
    While I can—and will—cook *you*!"

'So he boils the water, and takes the salt
    And the pepper in portions true
(Which he never forgot), and some chopped shalot,
    And some sage and parsley too.

' "Come here," says he, with a proper pride,
    Which his smiling features tell,
"'Twill soothing be if I let you see,
    How extremely nice you'll smell."

'And he stirred it round and round and round,
    And he sniffed at the foaming froth;
When I ups with his heels, and smothers his squeals
    In the scum of the boiling broth.

'And I eat that cook in a week or less,
    And—as I eating be
The last of his chops, why, I almost drops,
    For a wessel in sight I see!

'And I never grin, and I never smile,
    And I never larf nor play,
But I sit and croak, and a single joke
    I have—which is to say:

'Oh, I am a cook and a captain bold,
    And the mate of the *Nancy* brig,
*And* a bo'sun tight, *and* a midshipmite,
    *And* the crew of the captain's gig!'

W.S. GILBERT

## Country Places
*'Hell, Hay and Booligal!'—an old New South Wales saying*

I glean them from signposts in these country places,
Weird names, some beautiful, more that make me laugh.
Driving to fat-lamb sales or to picnic races,
I pass their worshippers of the golden calf

And, in the dust of their Cadillacs, a latter-day Habbakuk
Rises in me to preach comic sermons of doom,
Crying: 'Woe unto Tocumwal, Teddywaddy, Tooleybuc!'
And: 'Wicked Wallumburrawang, your hour has come!'

But when the Four Horsemen ride their final muster
And my sinful country sinks in fiery rain
One name shall survive the doom and the disaster
That fell on the foolish cities of the plain.
Like the three holy children or the salamander
One place shall sing and flourish in the fire:
It is Sweet Water Creek at Mullengandra
And there at the Last Day I shall retire.

When Numbugga shrieks to Burrumbuttock:
'The curse of Sodom comes upon us all!'
When Tumbarumba calls for spade and mattock
And they bury Hell and Hay in Booligal;
When the wrath of God is loosed upon Gilgandra
And Gulargambone burns red against the west,
To Sweet Water Creek at Mullengandra
I shall rise and flee away and be at rest.

When from Goonoo Goonoo, Underbool and Grong Grong
And Suggan Buggan there goes up the cry,
From Tittybong, Drik Drik and Drung Drung,
'Help, Lord, help us, or we die!'
I shall lie beside a willow-cool meander, or
Cut myself a fly-whisk in the shade
And from Sweet Water Creek at Mullengandra
Fill my cup and whet my whistle unafraid.

When Boinka lies in ruins (more's the pity!)
And a heavenly trump proclaims the end of Grace,
With: 'Wombat is fallen, is fallen, that great city!'
Adding: 'Bunyip is in little better case.'
When from Puckapunyal and from Yackandandah
The cry goes up: 'How long, O Lord, how long?'
I shall hear the she-oaks sough at Mullengandra
And the Sweet Waters ripple into song.

O, there's little to be hoped for Grabben Gullen
And Tumbulgum shrinks and shudders at its fate;
Folks at Wantabadgery and Cullen Bullen
Have Buckley's chance of reaching Heaven's gate;
It's all up with Cootamundra and Kiandra
And at Collarenebri they know they're through;
But at Sweet Water Creek at Mullengandra
You may pitch your camp and sleep the whole night through.

God shall punish Cargellico, Come-by-Chance, Chinkapook;
They shall dance no more at Merrijig nor drink at Gentleman's Halt;
The sin of Moombooldool He shall in no wise overlook;
Wee Jasper and Little Jilliby, He shall not condone their fault;
But though I preach down Nap Nap and annihilate Narrandera,
One place shall yet be saved, this I declare:
Sweet Water Creek at Mullengandra
For its name and for my sake the Lord shall spare.

A.D. HOPE

## The Traveller

As I rode in to Burrumbeet,
I met a man with funny feet;
And, when I paused to ask him why
His feet were strange, he rolled his eye
And said the rain would spoil the wheat;
So I rode on to Burrumbeet.

As I rode in to Beetaloo,
I met a man whose nose was blue;
And when I asked him how he got
A nose like that, he answered, 'What
Do bullocks mean when they say "Moo"?'
So I rode on to Beetaloo.

As I rode in to Ballarat,
I met a man who wore no hat;
And, when I said he might take cold,
He cried, 'The hills are quite as old
As yonder plains, but not so flat.'
So I rode on to Ballarat.

As I rode in to Gundagai,
I met a man and passed him by
Without a nod, without a word.
He turned, and said he'd never heard
Or seen a man so wise as I.
But I rode on to Gundagai.

As I rode homeward, full of doubt,
I met a stranger riding out:
A foolish man he seemed to me;
But, 'Nay, I am yourself,' said he,
'Just as you were when you rode out.'
So I rode homeward, free of doubt.

C.J. DENNIS

### Smiling Villain

Forth from his den to steal he stole,
His bags of chink he chunk,
And many a wicked smile he smole,
And many a wink he wunk.

ANON

### Cargoes

Quinquireme of Nineveh from distant Ophir
Rowing home to haven in sunny Palestine,
With a cargo of ivory,
And apes and peacocks,
Sandalwood, cedarwood, and sweet white wine.

Stately Spanish galleon coming from the Isthmus,
Dipping through the Tropics by the palm-green shores,
With a cargo of diamonds,
Emeralds, amethysts,
Topazes, and cinnamon, and gold moidores.

Dirty British coaster with a salt-caked smoke stack
Butting through the Channel in the mad March days,
With a cargo of Tyne coal,
Road-rail, pig-lead,
Firewood, iron-ware, and cheap tin trays.

JOHN   MASEFIELD

### Dahn the Plug-'ole

A muvver was barfin' 'er biby one night,
The youngest of ten and a tiny young mite,
The muvver was pore and the biby was thin,
Only a skelington covered in skin;
The muvver turned rahnd for the soap orf the rack,
She was but a moment, but when she turned back,
The biby was gorn; and in anguish she cried,
'Oh, where is my biby?' — The angels replied:
'Your biby 'as fell dahn the plug-'ole,
Your biby 'as gorn dahn the plug;
The poor little thing was so skinny and thin
'E oughter been barfed in a jug;
Your biby is perfeckly 'appy,
'E won't need a barf any more,
Your biby 'as fell dahn the plug-'ole,
Not lorst, but gorn before.'

ANON

### Here Lies a Poor Woman

Here lies a poor woman who always was tired,
    She lived in a house where no help wasn't hired,
The last words she said were 'Dear friends, I am going,
    Where washing an't wanted, nor mending, nor sewing.
There all things is done just exact to my wishes,
    For where folk don't eat there's no washing of dishes.
In Heaven loud anthems for ever are ringing,
    But having no voice, I'll keep clear of the singing.
Don't mourn for me now, don't mourn for me never;
    I'm going to do nothing for ever and ever.'

ANON

### Wishes of an Elderly Man

I wish I loved the Human Race;
I wish I loved its silly face;
I wish I liked the way it walks;
I wish I liked the way it talks;
And when I'm introduced to one
I wish I thought *What Jolly Fun!*

WALTER   RALEIGH

### The Tale of Lord Lovell

Lord Lovell he stood at his own front door,
    Seeking the hole for the key;
His hat was wrecked, and his trousers bore
    A rent across either knee,
When down came the beauteous Lady Jane
    In fair white draperie.

'Oh, where have you been, Lord Lovell?' she said,
    'Oh, where have you been?' said she;
'I have not closed an eye in bed,
    And the clock has just struck three.
Who has been standing you on your head
    In the ash-barrel, pardie?'

'I am not drunk, Lad' Shane,' he said:
    'And so late it cannot be;
The clock struck one as I entered—

I heard it two times or three;
It must be the salmon on which I fed
    Has been too many for me.'

'Go tell your tale, Lord Lovell,' she said,
    'To the maritime cavalree,
To your grandmother of the hoary head—
    To any one but me:
The door is not used to be opened
    With a cigarette for a key.'

ANON

## An Ew Erra

The typeriter is crating
A revlootion in peotry
Pishing back the frontears
And apening up fresh feels
Unherd of by Done or Bleak

Mine is a Swetish Maid
Called FACIT
Others are OLIMPYA or ARUSTOCART
RAMINTONG or LOLITEVVI

TAB e or not TAB e
i.e. the?
Tygirl tygirl burning bride
Y, this is L
Nor-my-outfit
Anywan can od it
U 2 can b a
Tepot

C! *** stares and /// strips
Cloaca nd †-
Farty-far keys to suckcess!
A banus of + % for all futre peots!!
LSD & $$$

The trypewiter is cretin
A revultion in peotry
" "All nem r =" "
O how they £ away
@UNDERWORDS and ALLIWETTIS
Without a.

    FACIT cry I! ! !

D.J. ENRIGHT

## Limericks

There once was a person from Lyme
Who married three wives at a time.
    When asked, 'Why a third?'
    He replied, 'One's absurd,
And bigamy, sir, is a crime.'

ANON

There was a young man of Oporta,
Who daily got shorter and shorter.
    The reason, he said,
    Was the hod on his head,
Which was filled with the heaviest mortar.

LEWIS   CARROLL

A man hired by John Smith and Co.
Loudly declared he would tho.
    Man that he saw
    Dumping dirt near his store.
The drivers, therefore, didn't do.

MARK   TWAIN

There was an old man of Thermopylae,
Who never did anything properly;
    But they said, 'If you choose
    To boil eggs in your shoes,
You shall never remain in Thermopylae.'

EDWARD   LEAR

## Five Clerihews

The Art of Biography
Is different from Geography.
Geography is about Maps,
But Biography is about Chaps.

Although Don Bradman
Screamed and fought like a madman
And condemned the proceedings *in toto*,
They insisted on taking his photo.

When I faced the bowling of Hirst
I ejaculated, 'Do your worst!'
He said, 'Right you are, Sid.'
—And he did.


George the Third
Ought never to have occurred.
One can only wonder
At so grotesque a blunder.


It was a rule of Leonardo da Vinci's
Not to put his trust in princes.
Pleading was of no avail;
They had to pay up on the nail.

EDMUND CLERIHEW BENTLEY


## On Mike O'Day

This is the grave of Mike O'Day
Who died maintaining his right of way.
His right was clear, his will was strong,
But he's just as dead as if he'd been wrong.

ANON


## On Martin Elginbrod

Here lie I, Martin Elginbrod.
Hae mercy on my soul, Lord God;
As I would do, were I Lord God,
And ye were Martin Elginbrod.

ANON


## Epitaph for William Pitt

With death doom'd to grapple,
  Beneath this cold slab, he
Who lied in the Chapel
  Now lies in the Abbey.

BYRON

### Epitaph on a Dentist

Stranger, approach this spot with gravity;
John Brown is filling his last cavity.

ANON

### The Nocturne in the Corner Phonebox

Someone is playing a trombone
in the telephone box outside my room.
It's 1 a.m.
and he's removed the globe.
He's playing a melancholy cadenza
probably over the S.T.D.
to his girl in Sydney.

I can imagine . . .
she's curled to the telephone
listening to that impossible music
a smile curving her face.
I wonder if he has enough change
for those extensions.
Could he reverse the charge?

Somebody called Hugh Adamson
blares out a nocturne in a phonebox.
His father's old and dying,
his mother's dead, his girl's away,
he's very sad, his nocturne's very sad,
his trombone blares and flares and says
'He's very sad, yair yair, he's very sad.'

Maybe he's only playing to a friend
in East St Kilda.
Maybe he hasn't any change.
Someone is playing a trombone—impossible—
in the phonebox with the door shut.
I've no idea who he is. I'm waiting
for my phone to ring. I like this music.

ANDREW  TAYLOR

### Jabberwocky

'Twas brillig, and the slithy toves
Did gyre and gimble in the wabe;
All mimsy were the borogroves,
And the mome raths outgrabe.

'Beware the Jabberwock, my son!
The jaws that bite, the claws that catch!
Beware the Jubjub bird and shun
The frumious Bandersnatch!'

He took his vorpal sword in hand:
Long time the manxome foe he sought—
So rested he by the Tumtum tree,
And stood awhile in thought.

And as in uffish thought he stood,
The Jabberwock, with eyes of flame,
Came whiffling through the tulgey wood,
And burbled as it came!

One, two! One, two! And through and through
The vorpal blade went snicker-snack!
He left it dead, and with its head
He went galumphing back.

'And hast thou slain the Jabberwock!
Come to my arms, my beamish boy!
O frabjous day! Callooh! Callay!'
He chortled in his joy.

'Twas brillig, and the slithy toves
Did gyre and gimble in the wabe;
All mimsy were the borogroves,
And the mome raths outgrabe.

LEWIS   CARROLL

## The Jumblies

They went to sea in a Sieve, they did,
   In a Sieve they went to sea:
In spite of all their friends could say,
On a winter's morn, on a stormy day,
   In a Sieve they went to sea!
And when the Sieve turned round and round,
And every one cried, 'You'll all be drowned!'
They called aloud, 'Our Sieve ain't big,
But we don't care a button ! we don't care a fig!
   In a Sieve we'll go to sea!'
      Far and few, far and few,
         Are the lands where the Jumblies live;
      Their heads are green, and their hands are blue,
         And they went to sea in a Sieve.

They sailed away in a Sieve, they did,
  In a Sieve they sailed so fast,
With only a beautiful pea-green veil
Tied with a riband by way of a sail,
  To a small tobacco-pipe mast;
And every one said, who saw them go,
'O won't they be soon upset, you know!
For the sky is dark, and the voyage is long,
And happen what may, it's extremely wrong
  In a Sieve to sail so fast!'
    Far and few, far and few,
      Are the lands where the Jumblies live;
    Their heads are green, and their hands are blue,
      And they went to sea in a Sieve.


The water it soon came in, it did,
  The water it soon came in;
So to keep them dry, they wrapped their feet
In a pinky paper all folded neat,
  And they fastened it down with a pin.
And they passed the night in a crockery-jar,
And each of them said, 'How wise we are!
Though the sky be dark, and the voyage be long,
Yet we never can think we were rash or wrong,
While round in our Sieve we spin!'
    Far and few, far and few,
      Are the lands where the Jumblies live;
    Their heads are green, and their hands are blue,
      And they went to sea in a Sieve.


And all night long they sailed away;
  And when the sun went down,
They whistled and warbled a moony song
To the echoing sound of a coppery gong,
  In the shade of the mountains brown.
'O Timballoo! How happy we are,
When we live in a Sieve and a crockery-jar,
And all night long in the moonlight pale,
We sail away with a pea-green sail,
  In the shade of the mountains brown!'
    Far and few, far and few,
      Are the lands where the Jumblies live;
    Their heads are green, and their hands are blue,
      And they went to sea in a Sieve.

They sailed to the Western Sea, they did,
   To a land all covered with trees,
And they bought an Owl, and a useful Cart,
And a pound of Rice, and a Cranberry Tart,
   And a hive of silvery Bees.
And they bought a Pig, and some green Jack-daws,
And a lovely Monkey with lollipop paws,
And forty bottles of Ring-Bo-Ree,
   And no end of Stilton Cheese.
     Far and few, far and few,
      Are the lands where the Jumblies live;
     Their heads are green, and their hands are blue,
      And they went to sea in a Sieve.


And in twenty years they all came back,
   In twenty years or more,
And every one said, 'How tall they've grown!
For they've been to the Lakes, and the Torrible Zone,
   And the hills of the Chankly Bore';
And they drank their health, and gave them a feast
Of dumplings made of beautiful yeast;
And every one said, 'If we only live,
We too will go to sea in a Sieve,—
   To the hills of the Chankly Bore!'
     Far and few, far and few,
      Are the lands where the Jumblies live;
     Their heads are green, and their hands are blue,
      And they went to sea in a Sieve.

EDWARD LEAR

# Ballads

The voice that speaks to us in the traditional ballad is the voice of a whole community, not the voice of an individual poet. The ballad takes us back in spirit to the origin of poetry itself when all poems were spoken or sung to a listening audience, not written down for solitary readers or set for essay topics or examination questions. Such anonymous oral poetry develops its own themes and traditions. These are related to the interests of the particular community, knightly conduct and romantic love in the case of the ancient English and Scots ballads, bushranging and defiance of the police in many nineteenth-century Australian ballads. The ballads also develop their own conventions and style connected with the best ways of holding an audience and stirring their emotions. Suspense, repetition, and a moral ending recur frequently in the ballads of all countries.

The ancient ballads celebrate the lives, loves and deaths of folk heroes with stark simplicity. 'The Bonnie Earl of Murray' is a brief poignant lament for a brave ('bra') Scottish lord, while 'Sir Patrick Spens' tells the story of a gallant sailor and his men who were drowned on a mission for the King of Scotland. Extreme economy is observed in the telling. Each ballad stanza is like a film shot that marks a new stage in the action, and the anonymous poet cuts economically from one scene to the next, leaving the audience to fill up the gaps with their imaginations. Even though the ballad is tragic, an ironic humour broods over the telling, as the poet notes how the Scottish lords who were too proud to get their shoes wet were totally submerged when the water came above their hats.

> But long ere all the play were played
> Their hats they swam aboon.

The four-line ballad stanza lends itself to a variety of effects: brisk plain narrative, vivid description, dramatic dialogue, and repeated lines and phrases that often crystallise the essence of the action or the emotional experience. Moreover, such repetitions as the following are especially appropriate for spoken delivery:

'Oh what is the matter?' Lord Lovel he said,
  'Oh what is the matter?' said he.

In Australia, the ballad has been used to celebrate the adventures of the folk heroes of the early pioneering days. 'Brave Ben Hall' is proudly Australian in its subject matter, language, and sentiments; but we might notice that its anonymous author specifically links his hero with the English highwayman Dick Turpin and uses the traditional four-line ballad stanza. In general, the Australian ballad is notable for its celebration of outlawry, its vigorous contempt for authority, its evocation of Bush scenery and manners, and its rough jaunty rhythms. The first stanza of 'West By North Again' is typical:

We've drunk our wine, we've kissed our girls, and funds are sinking low,
The horses must be thinking it's a fair thing now to go;
Sling the swags on Condamine and strap the billies fast,
And stuff a bottle in the bags and let's be off at last.

It is from such rough, long, ballad lines as these that most of us build up our picture of the Bush a hundred years ago.

In 'The Convict and the Lady', James McAuley proves that there is still life in the ballad form. Taking as his subject a traditional story connected with one of Hobart's historic churches, he combines atmosphere, vigorous narrative and humour.

### Sir Patrick Spens

The king sits in Dumferlin town
  Drinking the blood-red wine:
Oh where will I get a good sailor
  To sail this ship of mine?

Up and spake an eldern knight
  Sat at the king's right knee:
Sir Patrick Spens is the best sailor
  That sails upon the sea.

The king has written a broad letter
  And signed it with his hand,
And sent it to Sir Patrick Spens
  Was walking on the strand.

To Noroway, to Noroway,
  To Noroway o'er the foam,
The king's daughter to Noroway,
  'Tis thou maun bring her home.

The first line that Sir Patrick read
  A loud laugh laughed he;
The next line that Sir Patrick read
  A tear blinded his eye.

Oh who is this has done this deed,
  This ill deed done to me,
To send me out this time of the year
  To sail upon the sea?

Make haste, make haste, my merry men all;
  Our good ship sails the morn.
Oh say not so, my master dear,
  For I fear a deadly storm.

Late, late yestreen I saw the new moon
  With the old moon in her arm,
And I fear, I fear, my master dear,
  That we will come to harm.

They hadna sailed a league, a league,
  A league but barely three,
When the air grew dark, and the wind blew loud,
  And growly grew the sea.

Oh our Scotch nobles were right loth
  To wet their cork-heeled shoon,
But long ere all the play were played
  Their hats they swam aboon.

Oh long, long may their ladies sit
  With their fans into their hand
Ere ever they see Sir Patrick Spens
  Come sailing to the land.

Oh long, long may the ladies stand
  With their gold combs in their hair
Waiting for their own dear lords,
  For they'll see them no more.

Half o'er, half o'er to Aberdour
  It's fifty fathom deep,
And there lies good Sir Patrick Spens
  With the Scotch lords at his feet.

ANON

## The Bonnie Earl of Murray

Ye Highlands and ye Lawlands.
    Oh! where hae ye been?
They hae slain the Earl of Murray,
    And hae laid him on the green.

Now wae be to thee, Huntly,
    And wherefore did you sae?
I bade you bring him wi' you,
    But forbade you him to slay.

He was a braw gallant,
    And he rid at the ring;
And the bonnie Earl of Murray,
    Oh! he might hae been a king.

He was a braw gallant,
    And he play'd at the ba';
And the bonnie Earl of Murray
    Was the flower amang them a'.

He was a braw gallant,
    And he play'd at the glove;
And the bonnie Earl of Murray,
    Oh! he was the Queen's luve.

Oh! lang will his lady
    Look owre the castle Down,
Ere she see the Earl of Murray
    Come sounding thro' the town.

ANON

## Helen of Kirkconnell

I wish I were where Helen lies,
    Night and day on me she cries;
O that I were where Helen lies,
    On fair Kirkconnell lea!

Curst be the heart that thought the thought,
And curst the hand that fired the shot,
When in my arms burd Helen dropt,
    And died to succour me!

O think na ye my heart was sair,
When my Love dropp'd and spak nae mair!
There did she swoon wi' meikle care,
   On fair Kirkconnell lea.

As I went down the water side,
None but my foe to be my guide,
None but my foe to be my guide,
   On fair Kirkconnell lea;

I lighted down my sword to draw,
I hackèd him in pieces sma',
I hackèd him in pieces sma',
   For her sake that died for me.

O Helen fair, beyond compare!
I'll mak a garland o' thy hair,
Shall bind my heart for evermair,
   Until the day I dee!

O that I were where Helen lies!
Night and day on me she cries;
Out of my bed she bids me rise,
   Says, 'Haste, and come to me!'

O Helen fair! O Helen chaste!
If I were with thee, I'd be blest,
Where thou lies low and taks thy rest,
   On hair Kirkconnell lea.

I wish my gave were growing green,
A winding-sheet drawn owre my een,
And I in Helen's arms lying,
   On fair Kirkconnell lea.

I wish I were where Helen lies!
Night and day on me she cries;
And I am weary of the skies,
   For her sake that died for me

ANON

### Lord Lovel

Lord Lovel he stood at his castle-gate,
    Combing his milk-white steed,
When up came Lady Nancy Belle,
    To wish her lover good speed.

'Where are you going, Lord Lovel?' she said,
    'Oh where are you going?' said she.
'I'm going, my Lady Nancy Belle,
    Strange countries for to see.'

'When will you be back, Lord Lovel?' she said,
    'Oh when will you come back?' said she.
'In a year, or two, or three at the most,
    I'll return to my fair Nancỳ.'

But he had not been gone a year and a day,
    Strange countries for to see,
When languishing thoughts came into his head,
    Lady Nancy Belle he would go see.

So he rode, and he rode, on his milk-white steed,
    Till he came to London town,
And there he heard St. Pancras' bells,
    And the people all mourning round.

'Oh what is the matter?' Lord Lovel he said.
    'Oh what is the matter?' said he;
'A lord's lady is dead,' a woman replied,
    'And some call her Lady Nancỳ.'

So he order'd the grave to be open'd wide,
    And the shroud he turnèd down,
And there he kiss'd her clay-cold lips,
    Till the tears came trickling down.

Lady Nancy she died, as it might be, today,
    Lord Lovel he died as tomorrow;
Lady Nancy she died out of pure, pure grief,
    Lord Lovel he died out of sorrow.

Lady Nancy was laid in St. Pancras' Church,
    Lord Lovel was laid in the choir;
And out of her bosom there grew a red rose,
    And out of her lover's a briar.

They grew, and they grew, to the church-steeple top,
    And then they could grow no higher;
So there they entwined in a true-lovers' knot,
    For all lovers true to admire.

ANON

## How Gilbert Died

There's never a stone at the sleeper's head,
There's never a fence beside,
And the wandering stock on the grave may tread
Unnoticed and undenied;
But the smallest child on the Watershed
Can tell you how Gilbert died.

For he rode at dusk with his comrade Dunn
To the hut at the Stockman's Ford;
In the waning light of the sinking sun
They peered with a fierce accord.
They were outlaws both—and on each man's head
Was a thousand pounds reward.

They had taken toll of the country round,
And the troopers came behind
With a black that tracked like a human hound
In the scrub and the ranges blind:
He could run the trail where a white man's eye
No sign of a track could find.

He had hunted them out of the One Tree Hill
And over the Old Man Plain,
But they wheeled their tracks with a wild beast's skill,
And they made for the range again;
Then away to the hut where their grandsire dwelt
They rode with a loosened rein.

And their grandsire gave them a greeting bold:
'Come in and rest in peace,
No safer place does the country hold—
With the night pursuit must cease,
And we'll drink success to the roving boys,
And to hell with the black police.

But they went to death when they entered there
In the hut at the Stockman's Ford,
For their grandsire's words were as false as fair—
They were doomed to the hangman's cord.
He had sold them both to the black police
For the sake of the big reward.

In the depth of night there are forms that glide
As stealthy as serpents creep,
And around the hut where the outlaws hide
They plant in the shadows deep,
And they wait till the first faint flush of dawn
Shall waken their prey from sleep.

But Gilbert wakes while the night is dark—
A restless sleeper aye,
He has heard the sound of a sheep-dog's bark,
And his horse's warning neigh,
And he says to his mate, 'There are hawks abroad,
And it's time we went away.'

Their rifles stood at the stretcher head,
Their bridles lay to hand;
They wakened the old man out of his bed,
When they heard the sharp command:
'In the name of the Queen lay down your arms,
Now, Dunn and Gilbert, stand!'

Then Gilbert reached for his rifle true
That close at hand he kept;
He point straight at the voice, and drew,
But never a flash outleapt,
For the water ran from the rifle breech—
It was drenched while the outlaws slept.

Then he dropped the piece with a bitter oath,
And he turned to his comrade Dunn:
'We are sold,' he said, 'we are dead men both,
But there may be a chance for one;
I'll stop and I'll fight with the pistol here,
You take to your heels and run.'

So Dun crept out on his hands and knees
In the dim, half-dawning light,
And he made his way to a patch of trees,
And was lost in the black of night;
And the trackers hunted his tracks all day,
But they never could trace his flight.

But Gilbert walked from the open door
In a confident style, and rash;
He heard at his side the rifles roar,
And he heard the bullets crash.
But he laughed as he lifted his pistol-hand,
And he fired at the rifle flash.

Then out of the shadows the troopers aimed
At his voice and the pistol sound.
With rifle flashes the darkness flamed—
He staggered and spun around,
And they riddled his body with rifle balls
As it lay on the blood-soaked ground.

There's never a stone at the sleeper's head,
There's never a fence beside,

And the wandering stock on the grave may tread.
Unnoticed and undenied;
but the smallest child on the Watershed
Can tell you how Gilbert died.

A.B. ('BANJO') PATERSON

## West by North Again

We've drunk our wine, we've kissed our girls, and funds are sinking low,
The horses must be thinking it's a fair thing now to go;
Sling the swags on Condamine and strap the billies fast,
And stuff a bottle in the bags and let's be off at last.

What matter if the creeks are up—the cash, alas, runs down!
A very sure and certain sign we're long enough in town.
The nigger rides the boko, and you'd better take the bay,
Quart Pot will do to carry me the stage we go today.

No grass this side the Border fence! and all the mulga's dead!
The horses for a day or two will have to spiel ahead;
Man never yet from Queensland brought a bullock or a hack
But lost condition on that God-abandoned Border track.

When once we're through the rabbit-proof—it's certain since the rain—
There's whips o' grass and water, so, it's West by North again!
There's feed on Tyson's country—we can 'spell' the mokes a week
Where Billy Stevens last year trapped his brumbies on Bough Creek.

The Paroo may be quickly crossed—the Eulo Common's bare;
And, anyhow, it isn't wise, old man! to dally there.
Alack-a-day! far wiser men than you and I succumb
To woman's wiles, and potency of Queensland wayside rum.

Then over sand and spinifex and on, o'er ridge and plain!
The nags are fresh—besides, they know they're westward-bound again.
The brand upon old Darkie's thigh is that upon the hide
Of bullocks we must muster on the Diamantina side.

We'll light our camp-fires where we may, and yarn beside their blaze;
The jingling hobble-chains shall make a music through the days.
And while the tucker-bags are right, and we've a stick of weed,
A swagman shall be welcome to a pipe-full and a feed.

So, fill your pipe! and, ere we mount, we'll drink another nip—
Here's how that West by North again may prove a lucky trip;
Then back again—I trust you'll find your best girl's merry face,
Or, if she jilts you, may you get a better in her place.

HARRY MORANT

## Brave Ben Hall

Come all Australian sons with me
For a hero has been slain
And cowardly butchered in his sleep
Upon the Lachlan Plain.

Pray do not stay your seemly grief
But let a teardrop fall
For many hearts shall always mourn
The fate of bold Ben Hall.

No brand of Cain e'er stamped his brow,
No widow's curse did fall;
When tales are read the squatters dread
The name of bold Ben Hall.

The records of this hero bold
Through Europe have been heard,
And formed a conversation
Between many an Earl and Lord.

Ever since the good old days
Of Dick Turpin and Duval,
Knights of the road were outlaws bold,
And so was bold Ben Hall.

He never robbed a needy man,
His records best will show,
Staunch and loyal to his mates,
And manly to the foe.

Until he left his trusty mates,
The cause I ne'er could hear,
The bloodhounds of the law heard this
And after him did steer.

They found his place of ambush,
And cautiously they crept,
And savagely they murdered him
While the victim slept.

Yes, savagely they murdered him,
The cowardly blue-coat imps,
Who were laid onto where he slept
By informing peelers' pimps.

No more he'll mount his gallant steed,
Nor range the mountains high,
The widow's friend in poverty —
Bold Ben Hall, good-bye.

ANON

## The Ballad of Moll Magee

Come round me, little childer;
There, don't fling stones at me
Because I mutter as I go;
But pity Moll Magee.

My man was a poor fisher
With shore lines in the say;
My work was saltin' herrings
The whole of the long day.

And sometimes from the saltin' shed
I scarce could drag my feet,
Under the blessed moonlight,
Along the pebbly street.

I'd always been but weakly,
And my baby was just born;
A neighbour minded her by day,
I minded her till morn.

I lay upon my baby;
Ye little childer dear,
I looked on my cold baby
When the morn grew frosty and clear.

A weary woman sleeps so hard!
My man grew red and pale,
And gave me money, and bade me go
To my own place, Kinsale.

He drove me out and shut the door,
And gave his curse to me;
I went away in silence,
No neighbour could I see.

The windows and the doors were shut,
One star shone faint and green,
The little straws were turnin' round
Across the bare boreen.

I went away in silence:
Beyond old Martin's byre
I saw a kindly neighbour
Blowin' her mornin' fire.

She drew from me my story—
My money's all used up,
And still, with pityin', scornin' eye,
She gives me bite and sup.

She says my man will surely come
And fetch me home agin;
But always, as I'm movin' round,
Without doors or within,

Pilin' the wood or pilin' the turf,
Or goin' to the well,
I'm thinkin' of my baby
And keenin' to mysel'.

And sometimes I am sure she knows
When, openin' wide His door,
God lights the stars, His candles,
And looks upon the poor.

So now, ye little childer,
Ye won't fling stones at me;
But gather with your shinin' looks
And pity Moll Magee.

W.B. YEATS

**The Convict and the Lady**
*An incident in St George's Church, Battery Point*

Voluntaries of Clarke and Boyce
    Flow temperately sweet
With Gamba, Flute, and Clarabel,
And pedal Bourdon trampled well
    By shapely kid-skinned feet.

An apparition from the tower
    Suspends the diapason. —
Will she scream? No, courage wins,
And in that empty church begins
    An interesting liaison.

'Lady, I am a fugitive
    That's taken refuge here.
Up into the tower I crept,
Two days and nights I've waked and slept,
    But hunger masters fear.

'Now fetch me food, or fetch the law,
    For I am at your mercy.
Though forfeited in youthful spleen,
My birth and station were not mean,
    My name is Eustace Percy.'

So every day she brings her lunch,
    And practises the organ.
She finds him breeches, coat and vest,
And takes word to The Sailor's Rest,
    To a man named Harry Morgan.

One Sunday, as the lady plays
    'Recessional in A',
A stranger joins the genteel throng
That files out after Evensong;
    Unmarked, he slips away.

In darkness a small boat rows out
    Into the estuary.
The brig looms up upon the tide,
A shadow clambers up the side—
    And Eustace Percy's free!

So ends the tale? No, three years passed;
    From Hull a letter came:
'I thrive in my new way of life . . .'
The lady sailed to be his wife,
    And shared a borrowed name.

Organist, for that lady's sake,
    Select your stops and play
This postlude that I chose expressly,
By Samuel Sebastian Wesley,
    'Recessional in A'.

JAMES MCAULEY

# Songs

In Shakespeare's day and earlier, music and poetry were called the 'Sister Arts'. Poets were often musicians as well, and even when they were not they knew how to write poems that could be set to music and sung to the accompaniment of the lute, as in Wyatt's 'My Lute, Awake'. The songs they composed were written in the form of identical rhymed stanzas, so that each would fit the pattern and mood of the basic tune. The lines and phrases were also highly musical in themselves even when they were only spoken. Ben Jonson's 'Drink to me only', Donne's 'Sweetest Love I do not Go', and Ford's 'There is a Lady Sweet and Kind' are examples of this type of song. Its chief appeal is to our emotions and to our sense of pattern and harmony not to our intellect. A much later poet, Byron, shows that this tradition survived long after Shakespeare's day in his love songs 'So We'll Go No More A-Roving' and 'She Walks in Beauty', although by then the connection between music and poetry was not so strong. Shelley's poem 'To Night' retains the musically patterned stanza and echoing last lines of the older tradition known as the 'refrain'.

It would be quite impossible for anyone to set many of the poems in this section to music. They are 'Songs' in the sense that they are brief lyric poems, possessing a singing quality in their verbal rhythms such as we find in Macneice's 'The Sunlight on the Garden' and Judith Wright's 'The Man Beneath the Tree'. The most elaborate modern song in its intricate verbal rhythms is Dylan Thomas's 'Fern Hill'. The boyhood house is made part of the music by the use of the musical epithet 'lilting', a word normally applied to a tune. The repeated stanzas conform to a single intricate musical pattern, each having corresponding long and short lines. But, unlike the earlier writers of song, the Welsh poet does not employ rhyme to contribute to the musical effect and mark the end of the lines, but uses rather a subtle combination of alliteration, assonance, and lilting Welsh rhythms. These lines from the opening of the third stanza illustrate the careful patterning of the lines and the distinctive Welsh rhythms:

> All the sun long it was running, it was lovely, the hay
> Fields high as the house, the tunes from the chimneys, it was air
>   And playing, lovely and watery
>     And fire green as grass.

Two poems by Hardy, 'The Voice' and 'A Broken Appointment', are wonderful examples of a great modern poet's adaptation of rhymed stanza form to express a highly individual experience. The voice that speaks to us in most early songs is an impersonal voice expressing general truths about love and life, while the voice that speaks to us in Hardy and many other modern poets is more sharply individualised. It is worth noticing how the changed pattern and rhythm in the last four lines of 'The Voice' focus the sense of loss on the solitary tragic individual, whereas this sense has been more widely dispersed in the longer earlier lines:

> Thus I: faltering forward
> Leaves around me falling,
> Wind oozing thin through the thorn from norward,
>   And the woman calling.

In 'The Broken Appointment', the identical patterning of the two stanzas bestows an ordering calm on the grief expressed. This poem illustrates the general truth that poetic form enables a poet simultaneously to release and control deep emotion. It is not a decorative extra.

## There is a Lady Sweet and Kind

There is a Lady sweet and kind,
Was never face so pleased my mind;
I did but see her passing by,
And yet I love her till I die.

Her gesture, motion and her smiles,
Her wit, her voice, my heart beguiles,
Beguiles my heart, I know not why,
And yet I love her till I die.

Her free behaviour, winning looks,
Will make a lawyer burn his books.
I touched her not, alas, not I,
And yet I love her till I die.

Had I her fast betwixt mine arms,
Judge you that think such sports were harms
Wer't any harm? no, no, fie, fie!
For I will love her till I die.

Should I remain confined there,
So long as Phoebus in his sphere,
I to request, she to deny,
Yet would I love her till I die.

Cupid is wingèd and doth range,
Her country so my love doth change,
But change she earth, or change she sky,
Yet will I love her till I die.

THOMAS FORD

## My Lute, Awake!

My lute, awake! perform the last
Labour that thou and I shall waste,
    And end that I have now begun;
And when this song is sung and past,
    My lute, be still, for I have done.

As to be heard where ear is none,
As lead to grave in marble stone,
    My song may pierce her heart as soon.
Should we then sigh, or sing, or moan?
    No, no, my lute, for I have done.

The rocks do not so cruelly
Repulse the waves continually,
    As she my suit and affection;
So that I am past remedy,
    Whereby my lute and I have done.

Proud of the spoil that thou hast got
Of simple hearts thorough Love's shot,
    By whom, unkind, thou hast them won,
Think not he hath his bow forgot,
    Although my lute and I have done.

Vengeance shall fall on thy disdain,
That makest but game on earnest pain;
  Think not alone under the sun
Unquit to cause thy lovers plain,
  Although my lute and I have done.

May chance thee lie withered and old,
In winter nights that are so cold,
  Plaining in vain unto the moon;
Thy wishes then dare not be told.
  Care then who list, for I have done.

And then may chance thee to repent
The time that thou hast lost and spent
  To cause thy lovers sigh and swoon;
Then shalt thou know beauty but lent,
  And wish and want as I have done.

Now cease, my lute! this is the last
Labour that thou and I shall waste,
  And ended is that we begun;
Now is this song both sung and past.
  My lute, be still, for I have done.

SIR  THOMAS  WYATT

## So We'll Go No More A-Roving

So we'll go no more a-roving
  So late into the night,
Though the heart be still as loving,
  And the moon be still as bright.

For the sword outwears its sheath,
  And the soul wears out the breast,
And the heart must pause to breathe,
  And love itself have rest.

Though the night was made for loving,
  And the day returns too soon,
Yet we'll go no more a-roving
  By the light of the moon.

LORD  BYRON

## She Walks in Beauty

She walks in beauty, like the night
  Of cloudless climes and starry skies;
And all that's best of dark and bright
  Meet in her aspect and her eyes:
Thus mellowed to that tender light
  Which heaven to gaudy day denies.

One shade the more, one ray the less,
  Had half impaired the nameless grace,
Which waves in every raven tress,
  Or softly lightens o'er her face;
Where thoughts serenely sweet express
  How pure, how dear their dwelling-place.

And on that cheek, and o'er that brow,
  So soft, so calm, yet eloquent,
The smiles that win, the tints that glow,
  But tell of days in goodness spent,
A mind at peace with all below,
  A heart whose love is innocent!

LORD BYRON

## To Night

Swiftly walk o'er the western wave,
      Spirit of Night!
Out of the misty eastern cave,
Where, all the long and lone daylight,
Thou wovest dreams of joy and fear,
Which make thee terrible and dear, —
      Swift be thy flight!

Wrap thy form in a mantle gray,
      Star-inwrought!
Blind with thine hair the eyes of Day;
Kiss her until she be wearied out,
Then wander o'er city, and sea, and land,
Touching all with thine opiate wand—
      Come, long-sought!

When I arose and saw the dawn,
      I sighed for thee;
When light rode high, and the dew was gone,
And noon lay heavy on flower and tree,
And the weary Day turned to his rest,
Lingering like an unloved guest,
      I sighed for thee.

Thy brother Death came, and cried,
   Wouldst thou me?
Thy sweet child Sleep, the filmy-eyed,
Murmured like a noontide bee,
Shall I nestle near thy side?
Wouldst thou me?—And I replied,
   No, not thee!

Death will come when thou art dead,
   Soon, too soon—
Sleep will come when thou art fled;
Of neither would I ask the boon
I ask of thee, belovèd Night—
Swift be thine approaching flight,
   Come soon, soon!

       PERCY BYSSHE SHELLEY

## To Celia

Drink to me, only, with thine eyes,
And I will pledge with mine;
Or leave a kiss but in the cup,
And I'll not look for wine,
The thirst, that from the soul doth rise,
Doth ask a drink divine:
But might I of Jove's nectar sup,
I would not change for thine.
I sent thee, late, a rosy wreath,
Not so much honouring thee,
As giving it a hope, that there
It could not withered be.
But thou thereon did'st only breath,
And sent'st it back to me:
Since when it grows, and smells, I swear,
Not of itself, but thee.

       BEN JONSON

## To the Virgins, to Make Much of Time

Gather ye rose-buds while ye may,
Old Time is a still a flying:
And this same flower that smiles to day,
Tomorrow will be dying.

The glorious lamp of heaven, the sun,
The higher he's a getting;
The sooner will his race be run,
And nearer he's to setting.

That age is best, which is the first,
When youth and blood are warmer;
But being spent, the worse, and worst
Times, still succeed the former.

Then be not coy, but use your time;
And while ye may, go marry:
For having lost but once your prime,
You may for ever tarry.

ROBERT HERRICK

## Song

Sweetest love, I do not go,
    For weariness of thee,
Nor in hope the world can show
    A fitter love for me;
        But since that I
Must die at last, 'tis best,
To use myself in jest
    Thus by feigned deaths to die.

Yesternight the sun went hence,
    And yet is here today;
He hath no desire nor sense,
    Nor half so short a way;
        Then fear not me,
But believe that I shall make
Speedier journeys, since I take
    More wings and spurs than he.

O how feeble is man's power,
    That if good fortune fall,
Cannot add another hour,
    Nor a lost hour recall!
        But come bad chance,
And we join to it our strength,
And we teach it art and length,
    Itself o'er us to advance.

When thou sigh'st, thou sigh'st not wind,
   But sigh'st my soul away;
When thou weep'st, unkindly kind,
   My life's blood doth decay.
     It cannot be
That thou lovest me as thou say'st,
If in thine my life thou waste,
   That art the best of me.

Let not thy divining heart
   Forethink me any ill,
Destiny may take thy part,
   And may thy fears fulfil;
     But think that we
Are but turn'd aside to sleep;
They who one another keep
   Alive, ne'er parted be.

JOHN  DONNE

## The Message

Send home my long strayed eyes to me,
Which O! too long have dwelt on thee;
Yet since there they have learned such ill,
    Such forced fashions
    And false passions,
      That they be
      Made by thee
Fit for no good sight, keep them still.

Send home my harmless heart again,
Which no unworthy thought could stain;
But if it be taught by thine
    To make jestings
    Of protestings,
      And cross both
      Word and oath,
Keep it, for then 'tis none of mine.

Yet send me back my heart and eyes,
That I may know, and see thy lies,
And may laugh and joy, when thou
    Art in anguish
    And dost languish
      For some one
      That will none,
Or prove as false as thou art now.

JOHN  DONNE

## A Broken Appointment

           You did not come,
And marching Time drew on, and wore me numb. —
Yet less for loss of your dear presence there
Than that I thus found lacking in your make
That high compassion which can overbear
Reluctance for pure lovingkindness' sake
Grieved I, when, as the hope-hour stroked its sum,
           You did not come.

           You love not me,
And love alone can lend you loyalty;
—I know and knew it. But, unto the store
Of human deeds divine in all but name,
Was it not worth a little hour or more
To add yet this: Once you, a woman, came
To soothe a time-torn man; even though it be
           You love not me?

                THOMAS HARDY

## The Voice

Woman much missed, how you call to me, call to me,
Saying that now you are not as you were
When you had changed from the one who was all to me,
But as at first, when our day was fair.

Can it be you that I hear? Let me view you, then,
Standing as when I drew near to the town
Where you would wait for me: yes, as I knew you then,
Even to the original air-blue gown!

Or is it only the breeze, in its listlessness
Travelling across the wet mead to me here,
You being ever dissolved to wan wistlessness,
Heard no more again far or near?

      Thus I; faltering forward,
      Leaves around me falling,
Wind oozing thin through the thorn from norward,
      And the woman calling.

                THOMAS HARDY

## Death the Leveller

The glories of our blood and state
  Are shadows, not substantial things;
There is no armour against Fate;
  Death lays his icy hand on kings:
    Sceptre and Crown
    Must tumble down,
And in the dust be equal made
With the poor crooked scythe and spade.

Some men with swords may reap the field,
  And plant fresh laurels where they kill:
But their strong nerves at last must yield;
  They tame but one another still:
    Early or late
    They stoop to fate,
And must give up their murmuring breath
When they, pale captives, creep to death.

The garlands wither on your brow;
  Then boast no more your mighty deeds!
Upon Death's purple altar now
  See where the victor-victim bleeds.
    Your heads must come
    To the cold tomb:
Only the actions of the just
Smell sweet and blossom in their dust.

JAMES   SHIRLEY

## A Sea-Song

A wet sheet and a flowing sea,
  A wind that follows fast
And fills the white and rustling sail
  And bends the gallant mast;
And bends the gallant mast, my boys,
  While like the eagle free
Away the good ship flies, and leaves
  Old England on the lee.

O for a soft and gentle wind!
  I heard a fair one cry:
But give to me the snoring breeze
  And white waves heaving high;
And white waves heaving high, my lads,
  The good ship tight and free—
The world of waters is our home,
  And merry men are we.

There's tempest in yon hornèd moon,
    And lightning in yon cloud;
But hark the music, mariners!
    The wind is piping loud;

The wind is piping loud, my boys,
    The lightning flashes free—
While the hollow oak our palace is,
    Our heritage the sea.

ALLAN  CUNNINGHAM

## Idyll

Hermit hoar, in solemn cell,
    Wearing out life's evening grey,
Strike thy bosom, Sage, and tell
    What is bliss, and which the way.

Thus I spoke, and speaking sighed,
    Scarce repressed the starting tear,
When the hoary sage replied,
    'Come, my lad, and drink some beer.'

SAMUEL  JOHNSON

## Humping the Drum

I humped my drum from Kingdom Come
To the back of the Milky Way,
I boiled my quart on the Cape of York,
And I starved last Christmas Day.

I cast a line on the Condamine
And one on the Nebine Creek;
I've driven through bog, so help me bob,
Up Mungindi's main street;

I crossed the Murray and drank in Cloncurry
Where they charged a bob a nip.
I worked in the Gulf where the cattle they duff,
And the squatters let them rip.

I worked from morn in the fields of corn
Till the sun was out of sight,
I've cause to know the Great Byno,
And the Great Australian Bight.

I danced with Kit, when the lamps were lit,
And Doll, as the dance broke up;
I flung my hat on the myall track
When Bowman won the Cup.

I courted Flo in Jericho,
And Jane at old Blackall,
I said farewell to the Sydney belle
At the doors of the Eulo hall.

I laughed aloud in the merry crowd
In the city of the plains;
I sweated too on Ondooroo
While bogged in the big bore-drains.

I pushed my bike from the shearers' strike
Not wanting a funeral shroud;
I made the weights for the Flying Stakes
And I dodged the lynching crowd.

I've seen and heard upon my word,
Some strange things on my way,
But spare my days, I was knocked sideways
When I landed here today.

ANON

## A Short Song of Congratulation

Long-expected One-and-twenty,
  Lingering year, at length is flown:
Pride and pleasure, pomp and plenty,
  Great Sir John, are now your own.

Loosened from the minor's tether,
  Free to mortgage or to sell,
Wild as wind and light as feather,
  Bid the sons of thrift farewell.

Call the Betsies, Kates, and Jennies,
  All the names that banish care;
Lavish of your grandsire's guineas,
  Show the spirit of an heir.

All that prey on vice and folly
  Joy to see their quarry fly:
There the gamester, light and jolly,
  There the lender, grave and sly.

Wealth, my lad, was made to wander,
    Let it wander as it will;
Call the jockey, call the pander,
    Bid them come and take their fill.

When the bonny blade carouses,
    Pockets full, and spirits high—
What are acres? What are houses?
    Only dirt, or wet or dry.

Should the guardian friend or mother
    Tell the woes of wilful waste,
Scorn their counsel, scorn their pother;—
    You can hang or drown at last!

SAMUEL   JOHNSON

## The Man Beneath the Tree

Nothing is so far as truth;
nothing is so plain to see.
Look where light has married earth
through the green leaves on the tree.

Nothing is so hard as love—
love for which the wisest weep;
yet the child who never looked
found it easily as his sleep.

Nothing is as strange as love—
love is like a foreign land.
Yet its natives find their way
natural as hand-in-hand.

Nothing is so bare as truth—
that lean geometry of thought;
but round its poles there congregate
all foliage, flowers and fruits of earth.

Oh, love and truth and I should meet,
sighed the man beneath the tree;
but where should our acquaintance be?
Between your hat and the soles of your feet,
sang the bird on top of the tree.

JUDITH   WRIGHT

## Lay Your Sleeping Head

Lay your sleeping head, my love,
Human on my faithless arm;
Time and fevers burn away
Individual beauty from
Thoughtful children, and the grave
Proves the child ephemeral:
But in my arms till break of day
Let the living creature lie,
Mortal, guilty, but to me
The entirely beautiful.

Soul and body have no bounds:
To lovers as they lie upon
Her tolerant enchanted slope
In their ordinary swoon,
Grave the vision Venus sends
Of supernatural sympathy,
Universal love and hope;
While an abstract insight wakes
Among the glaciers and the rocks
The hermit's sensual ecstasy.

Certainty, fidelity
On the stroke of midnight pass
Like vibrations of a bell,
And fashionable madmen raise
Their pedantic boring cry;
Every farthing of the cost
All the dreaded cards foretell
Shall be paid, but from this night
Not a whisper, not a thought,
Not a kiss nor look be lost.

Beauty, midnight, vision dies:
Let the winds of dawn that blow
Softly round your dreaming head
Such a day of sweetness show
Eye and knocking heart may bless,
Find the mortal world enough;
Noons of dryness see you fed
By the involuntary powers,
Nights of insult let you pass
Watched by every human love.

W.H. AUDEN

## Delight in Disorder

A sweet disorder in the dress
Kindles in clothes a wantonness:
A lawn about the shoulders thrown
Into a fine distraction:
An erring lace, which here and there
Enthralls the crimson stomacher:
A cuff neglectful, and thereby
Ribbands to flow confusedly:
A winning wave (deserving note)
In the tempestuous petticoat:
A careless shoe-string, in whose tie
I see a wild civility:
Do more bewitch me, than when art
Is too precise in every part.

ROBERT  HERRICK

## Song—to Celia

Come my Celia, let us prove,
While we may, the sports of love;
Time will not be ours for ever:
He, at length, our good will sever.
Spend not then his gifts in vain.
Suns that set, may rise again:
But, if once we lose this light,
'Tis, with us, perpetual night.
Why should we defer our joys?
Fame, and rumour are but toys.
Cannot we delude the eyes
Of a few poor household spies?
Or his easier ears beguile,
So removed by our wile?
'Tis no sin, love's fruit to steal,
But the sweet theft to reveal:
To be taken, to be seen,
These have crimes accounted been.

BEN  JONSON

## The Sunlight on the Garden

The sunlight on the garden
Hardens and grows cold,
We cannot cage the minute
Within its nets of gold,
When all is told
We cannot beg for pardon.

Our freedom as free lances
Advances towards its end;
The earth compels, upon it
Sonnets and birds descend;
And soon, my friend,
We shall have no time for dances.

The sky was good for flying
Defying the church bells
And every evil iron
Siren and what it tells:
The earth compels,
We are dying, Egypt, dying.

And not expecting pardon,
Hardened in heart anew,
But glad to have sat under
Thunder and rain with you,
And grateful too
For sunlight on the garden.

LOUIS  MACNEICE

## Sic Vita

Like to the falling of a Star;
Or as the flights of eagles are;
Or like the fresh springs gaudy hue;
Or silver drops of morning dew;
Or like a wind that chafes the flood;
Or bubbles which on water stood;
Even such is man, whose borrowed light
Is straight called in, and paid to night.
 The wind blows out; the bubble dies;
 The spring entombed in autumn lies;
 The dew dries up; the star is shot;
 The flight is past; and Man forgot.

HENRY  KING

## Chanson Innocente

in Just-
spring     when the world is mud-
luscious the little
lame balloonman

whistles     far     and wee

and eddieandbill come
running from marbles and
piracies and it's
spring

when the world is puddle-wonderful

the queer
old balloonman whistles
far     and     wee
and bettyandisbel come dancing
from hop-scotch and jump-rope and

it's
spring
and
     the

          goat-footed

balloonMan     whistles
far
and
wee

E.E. CUMMINGS

## The Solitary Reaper

Behold her, single in the field,
Yon solitary highland lass!
Reaping and singing by herself;
Stop here, or gently pass!
Alone she cuts and binds the grain,
And sings a melancholy strain;
O listen! for the vale profound
Is overflowing with the sound.

No nightingale did ever chaunt
More welcome notes to weary bands
Of travellers in some shady haunt,
Among Arabian sands:
A voice so thrilling ne'er was heard
In spring-time from the cuckoo-bird,
Breaking the silence of the seas
Among the farthest Hebrides.

Will no one tell me what she sings?
Perhaps the plaintive numbers flow
For old, unhappy, far-off things,
And battles long ago:
Or is it some more humble lay,
Familiar matter of today?
Some natural sorrow, loss, or pain,
That has been, and may be again?

Whate'er the theme, the maiden sang
As if her song could have no ending;
I saw her singing at her work
And o'er the sickle bending;—
I listened, motionless and still;
And, as I mounted up the hill,
The music in my heart I bore,
Long after it was heard no more.

WILLIAM   WORDSWORTH

## Fern Hill

Now as I was young and easy under the apple boughs
About the lilting house and happy as the grass was green,
    The night above the dingle starry,
        Time let me hail and climb
    Golden in the heydays of his eyes,
And honoured among wagons I was prince of the apple towns
And once below a time I lordly had the trees and leaves
        Trail with daisies and barley
    Down the rivers of the windfall light.

And as I was green and carefree, famous among the barns
About the happy yard and singing as the farm was home,
    In the sun that is young once only,
        Time let me play and be
    Golden in the mercy of his means,
And green and golden I was huntsman and herdsman, the calves
Sang to my horn, the foxes on the hills barked clear and cold,
        And the sabbath rang slowly
    In the pebbles of the holy streams.

All the sun long it was running, it was lovely, the hay
Fields high as the house, the tunes from the chimneys, it was air
    And playing, lovely and watery
        And fire green as grass.
    And nightly under the simple stars
As I rode to sleep the owls were bearing the farm away,
All the moon long I heard, blessed among stables, the nightjars
    Flying with the ricks, and the horses
        Flashing into the dark.

And then to awake, and the farm, like a wanderer white
With the dew, come back, the cock on his shoulder: it was all
    Shining, it was Adam and maiden,
        The sky gathered again
    And the sun grew round that very day.
So it must have been after the birth of the simple light
In the first, spinning place, the spellbound horses walking warm
    Out of the whinnying green stable
        On to the fields of praise.

And honoured among foxes and pheasants by the gay house
Under the new made clouds and happy as the heart was long,
    In the sun born over and over,
        I ran my heedless ways,
    My wishes raced through the house high hay
And nothing I cared, at my sky blue trades, that time allows
In all his tuneful turning so few and such morning songs
    Before the children green and golden
        Follow him out of grace,

Nothing I cared, in the lamb white days, that time would
  take me
Up to the swallow thronged loft by the shadow of my hand,
    In the moon that is always rising,
        Nor that riding to sleep
    I should hear him fly with the high fields
And wake to the farm forever fled from the childless land.
Oh as I was young and easy in the mercy of his means,
        Time held me green and dying
    Though I sang in my chains like the sea.

DYLAN THOMAS

# Sonnets

One pattern that has continued to attract poets since it was first introduced into England from Italy in the sixteenth century is the sonnet. Within its fourteen lines and strict rhyme scheme poets discovered that they could control and shape the most intense and complicated emotions. Drayton's sonnet 'Since there's no help, come, let us kiss and part' and Shakespeare's 'Shall I compare thee to a summer's day' illustrate how the form was first used for love poetry, while Donne's 'Thou hast made me, and shall thy work decay?' and Shakespeare's 'Since brass, nor stone, nor earth nor boundless sea' reveal the great potential of the sonnet for serious meditations on time and man's mortality.

> O fearful meditation, where alack
> Shall Time's best jewel from Time's chest lie hid?

In a century of bitter religious controversy and civil war, the puritan poet John Milton extended the range of the sonnet still further by writing on burning political issues, as in his sonnet 'On the Late Massacre in Piedmont', a poem that calls for divine retribution on 'The bloody Piedmontese' who had slain the puritan martyrs. In his political sonnet, 'Europe', the contemporary Australian poet John Tranter shows that the sonnet tradition is still very much alive. So, too, do his countrymen Bruce Dawe and John Blight, while both Tranter and W.H. Auden demonstrate the way twentieth-century poets have given a modern air to the sonnet by retaining the basic fourteen-line shape but discarding any formal rhyme scheme.

The sonnet has always been a favourite form of expression for intense personal emotion. Milton's sonnet 'On his Blindness', Keats's 'When I have fears that I may cease to be' and Coleridge's 'Work Without Hope' all express moments of extreme crisis in the lives of the three poets. The ordered structure of the sonnets conveys the pattern the poets discover in their inner lives, as they confront spiritual realities and finally become reconciled to the sense of loss expressed in the opening lines. Thus Milton becomes reconciled to his loss of sight as he moves from a mood of dejection and futility to patient acquiescence in the will of God.

> 'Doth God exact day-labour, light denied?'
> I fondly ask; but patience to prevent
> That murmur, soon replies, 'God doth not need
> Either man's works or his own gifts, who best
> Bear his mild yoke, they serve him best, his state
> Is Kingly. Thousands at his bidding speed
> And post o'er land and ocean without rest:
> They also serve who only stand and wait.'

But for Keats and Coleridge there is no similar religious solution. Nevertheless, we feel that these two poets through writing their sonnets have passed from moods of dejection to states of greater vision and deeper understanding. Thus Keats's sonnet on the fear of death ends:

> then on the shore
> Of the wide world I stand alone, and think
> Till love and fame to nothingness do sink.

The sonnets in the following section provide ample proof that a strict verse form is not the enemy of truth but one of the means of achieving it.

### Since There's No Help

Since there's no help, come, let us kiss and part,
Nay, I have done, you get no more of me,
And I am glad, yea, glad with all my heart,
That thus so cleanly I myself can free.
Shake hands for ever, cancel all our vows,
And when we meet at any time again,
Be it not seen in either of our brows
That we one jot of former love retain.
Now at the last gasp of Love's latest breath,
When his pulse failing, Passion speechless lies,
When Faith is kneeling by his bed of death,
And Innocence is closing up his eyes,
Now, if thou wouldst, when all have given him over,
From death to life thou might'st him ye recover.

MICHAEL DRAYTON

## Shall I Compare Thee

Shall I compare thee to a summer's day?
Thou art more lovely and more temperate:
Rough winds do shake the darling buds of May,
And summer's lease hath all too short a date:
Sometime too hot the eye of heaven shines,
And often is his gold complexion dimmed,
And every fair from fair sometime declines,
By chance, or nature's changing course untrimmed:
But thy eternal summer shall not fade,
Nor lose possession of that fair thou ow'st,
Nor shall death brag thou wand'rest in his shade,
When in eternal lines to time thou grow'st,
    So long as men can breathe or eyes can see,
    So long lives this, and this gives life to thee.

WILLIAM SHAKESPEARE

## Let Me Not to the Marriage

Let me not to the marriage of true minds
Admit impediments, love is not love
Which alters when it alteration finds,
Or bends with the remover to remove.
O no, it is an ever-fixéd mark
That looks on tempests and is never shaken;
It is the star to every wand'ring bark,
Whose worth's unknown, although is height be taken.
Love's not Time's fool, though rosy lips and cheeks
Within his bending sickle's compass come,
Love alters not with his brief hours and weeks,
But bears it out even to the edge of doom:
    If this be error and upon me proved,
    I never writ, nor no man ever loved.

WILLIAM SHAKESPEARE

## When in Disgrace

When in disgrace with Fortune and men's eyes;
I all alone beweep my outcast state,
And trouble deaf Heaven with my bootless cries,
And look upon myself and curse my fate,
Wishing me like to one more rich in hope,
Featured like him, like him with friends possessed,
Desiring this man's art, and that man's scope,

With what I most enjoy contented least,
Yet in these thoughts myself almost despising,
Haply I think on thee, and then my state
(Like to the lark at break of day arising),
From sullen earth sings hymns at Heaven's gate,
For thy sweet love remembered such wealth brings,
That then I scorn to change my state with kings.

WILLIAM   SHAKESPEARE

### Since Brass, nor Stone

Since brass, nor stone, nor earth, nor boundless sea,
But sad mortality o'ersways their power,
How with this rage shall beauty hold a plea,
Whose action is no stronger than a flower?
O how shall summer's honey breath hold out,
Against the wrackful siege of batt'ring days,
When rocks impregnable are not so stout,
Nor gates of steel so strong but time decays?
O fearful meditation, where alack,
Shall Time's best jewel from Time's chest lie hid?
Or what strong hand can hold his swift foot back,
Or who his spoil of beauty can forbid?
    O none, unless this miracle have might,
    That in black ink my love may still shine bright.

WILLIAM   SHAKESPEARE

### That Time of Year

That time of year thou mayst in me behold,
When yellow leaves, or none, or few do hang
Upon those boughs which shake against the cold,
Bare ruined choirs, where late the sweet birds sang.
In me thou seest the twilight of such day,
As after sunset fadeth in the west,
Which by and by black night doth take away,
Death's second self that seals up all in rest.
In me thou seest the glowing of such fire,
That on the ashes of his youth doth lie,
As the death-bed, whereto it must expire,
Consumed with that which it was nourished by.
    This thou perceiv'st, which makes thy love more strong,
    To love that well, which thou must leave ere long.

WILLIAM   SHAKESPEARE

## Death Be Not Proud

Death be not proud, though some have callèd thee
Mighty and dreadful, for, thou art not so,
For, those whom thou think'st thou dost overthrow
Die not, poor death, nor yet canst thou kill me.
From rest and sleep, which but thy pictures be,
Much pleasure, then from thee much more must flow,
And soonest our best men with thee do go,
Rest of their bones, and soul's delivery.
Thou art slave to fate, chance, kings, and desperate men,
And dost with poison, war, and sickness dwell,
And poppy, or charms can make us sleep as well,
And better than thy stroke; why swell'st thou then?
One short sleep past, we wake eternally,
And death shall be no more; death, thou shalt die.

JOHN DONNE


## Thou Hast Made Me

Thou hast made me, and shall thy work decay?
Repair me now, for now mine end doth haste,
I run to death, and death meets me as fast,
And all my pleasures are like yesterday;
I dare not move my dim eyes any way,
Despair behind, and death before doth cast
Such terror, and my feeble flesh doth waste
By sin in it, which it towards hell doth weigh;
Only thou art above, and when towards thee
By thy leave I can look, I rise again;
But our old subtle foe so tempteth me,
That not one hour myself I can sustain;
Thy Grace may wing me to prevent his art,
And thou like adamant draw mine iron heart.

JOHN DONNE


## On His Blindness

When I consider how my light is spent,
Ere half my days, in this dark world and wide,
And that one talent which is death to hide,
Lodged with me useless, though my soul more bent
To serve therewith my Maker, and present
My true account, lest he returning chide,
'Doth God exact day-labour, light denied?'

I fondly ask; but patience to prevent
That murmur, soon replies, 'God doth not need
Either man's work or his own gifts, who best
Bear his mild yoke, they serve him best, his state
Is Kingly. Thousands at his bidding speed
And post o'er land and ocean without rest:
They also serve who only stand and wait.'

JOHN  MILTON

## On the Late Massacre in Piedmont

Avenge O Lord thy slaughtered Saints, whose bones
Lie scattered on the Alpine mountains cold,
Even them who kept thy truth so pure of old
When all our fathers worshipped stocks and stones,
Forget not: in thy book record their groans
Who were thy sheep and in their ancient fold
Slain by the bloody Piedmontese that rolled
Mother with infant down the rocks. Their moans
The vales redoubled to the hills, and they
To Heaven. Their martyred blood and ashes sow
O'er all the Italian fields where still doth sway
The triple Tyrant: that from these may grow
A hundred-fold, who having learnt thy way
Early may fly the Babylonian woe.

JOHN  MILTON

## Work without Hope

All Nature seems at work. Slugs leave their lair—
The bees are stirring—birds are on the wing—
And Winter slumbering in the open air,
Wears on his smiling face a dream of Spring!
And I, the while, the sole unbusy thing,
Nor honey make, nor pair, nor build, nor sing.
Yet well I ken the banks where amaranths blow,
Have traced the fount whence streams of nectar flow.
Bloom, O ye amaranths! bloom for whom ye may,
For me ye bloom not! Glide, rich streams, away!
With lips unbrightened, wreathless brow, I stroll:
And would you learn the spells that drowse my soul?
Work without hope draws nectar in a sieve,
And hope without an object cannot live.

SAMUEL  TAYLOR  COLERIDGE

## When I Have Fears

When I have fears that I may cease to be
Before my pen has gleaned my teeming brain,
Before high-pilèd books, in charactery,
Hold like rich garners the full ripened grain;
When I behold, upon the night's starred face,
Huge cloudy symbols of a high romance,
And think that I may never live to trace
Their shadows, with the magic hand of chance;
And when I feel, fair creature of an hour,
That I shall never look upon thee more,
Never have relish in the faery power
Of unreflecting love; — then on the shore
Of the wide world I stand alone, and think
Till love and fame to nothingness do sink.

JOHN KEATS

## A Prayer

Searcher of souls, you who in heaven abide,
To whom the secrets of all hearts are open,
Though I do lie to all the world beside,
From me to thee no falsehood shall be spoken.
Cleanse me not, Lord, I say, from secret sin
But from those faults which he who runs can see.
'Tis these that torture me, O Lord, begin
With these and let the hidden vices be;
If you must cleanse these too, at any rate
Deal with the seen sins first, 'tis only reason,
They being so gross, to let the others wait
The leisure of some more convenient season;
    And cleanse not all even then, leave me a few,
    I would not be—not quite—so pure as you.

SAMUEL BUTLER

## As Kingfishers Catch Fire

As kingfishers catch fire, dragonflies dráw fláme;
As tumbled over rim in roundy wells
Stones ring; like each tucked string tells, each hung bell's
Bow swung finds tongue to fling out broad its name;
Each mortal thing does one thing and the same:
Deals out that being indoors each one dwells;
Selves—goes itself; *myself* it speaks and spells;
Crying *Whát I dó is me: for that I came.*

Í say móre: the just man justices;
Kéeps gráce: thát keeps all his goings graces;
Acts in God's eye what in God's eye he is—
Christ—for Christ plays in ten thousand places,
Lovely in limbs, and lovely in eyes not his
To the Father through the features of men's faces.

GERARD MANLEY HOPKINS

## Peace

Now, God be thanked Who has matched us with His hour,
And caught our youth, and wakened us from sleeping,
With hand made sure, clear eye, and sharpened power,
To turn, as swimmers into cleanness leaping,
Glad from a world grown old and cold and weary,
Leave the sick hearts that honour could not move,
And half-men, and their dirty songs and dreary,
And all the little emptiness of love!

Oh! we, who have known shame, we have found release there,
Where there's no ill, no grief, but sleep has mending,
Naught broken save this body, lost but breath;
Nothing to shake the laughing heart's long peace there
But only agony, and that has ending;
And the worst friend and enemy is but Death.

RUPERT BROOKE

## Anthem for Doomed Youth

What passing-bells for these who die as cattle?
    Only the monstrous anger of the guns.
    Only the stuttering rifles' rapid rattle
Can patter out their hasty orisons.
No mockeries now for them; no prayers nor bells,
    Nor any voice of mourning save the choirs,—
The shrill, demented choirs of wailing shells;
    And bugles calling for them from sad shires.

What candles may be held to speed them all?
    Not in the hands of boys, but in their eyes
Shall shine the holy glimmers of good-byes.
    The pallor of girls' brows shall be their pall;
Their flowers the tenderness of patient minds,
And each slow dusk a drawing-down of blinds.

WILFRED OWEN

## When Serpents Bargain

when serpents bargain for the right to squirm
and the sun strikes to gain a living wage—
when thorns regard their roses with alarm
and rainbows are insured against old age

when every thrush may sing no new moon in
if all screech-owls have not okayed his voice
—and any wave signs on the dotted line
or else an ocean is compelled to close

when the oak begs permission of the birch
to make an acorn—valleys accuse their
mountains of having altitude—and march
denounces april as a saboteur

then we'll believe in that incredible
unanimal mankind (and not until)

E.E. CUMMINGS

## The Secret Agent

Control of the passes was, he saw, the key
To this new district, but who would get it?
He, the trained spy, had walked into the trap
For a bogus guide, seduced by the old tricks.

At Greenhearth was a fine site for a dam
And easy power, had they pushed the rail
Some stations nearer. They ignored his wires:
The bridges were unbuilt and trouble coming.

The street music seemed gracious now to one
For weeks up in the desert. Woken by water
Running away in the dark, he often had
Reproached the night for a companion
Dreamed of already. They would shoot, of course,
Parting easily two that were never joined.

W.H. AUDEN

## Death of a Whale

When the mouse died, there was a sort of pity:
the tiny, delicate creature made for grief.
Yesterday, instead, the dead whale on the reef
drew an excited multitude to the jetty.
How must a whale die to wring a tear?
Lugubrious death of a whale: the big
feast for the gulls and sharks; the tug
of the tide simulating life still there,
until the air, polluted, swings this way
like a door ajar from a slaughterhouse.
Pooh! pooh! spare us, give us the death of a mouse
by its tiny hole; not this in our lovely bay.
—Sorry, we are, too, when a child dies;
but at the immolation of a race, who cries?

JOHN   BLIGHT

## Suburban Sonnet

She practises a fugue, though it can matter
to no one now if she plays well or not.
Beside her on the floor two children chatter,
then scream and fight. She hushes them. A pot
boils over. As she rushes to the stove
too late, a wave of nausea overpowers
subject and counter-subject. Zest and love
drain out with soapy water as she scours
the crusted milk. Her veins ache. Once she played
for Rubinstein, who yawned. The children caper
round a sprung mousetrap where a mouse lies dead.
When the soft corpse won't move they seem afraid.
She comforts them; and wraps it in a paper
featuring: *Tasty dishes from stale bread.*

GWEN   HARWOOD

## Migrants

In the fourth week the sea dropped clear away
And they were there . . .
                                    At first the people's slurred
Indifference surprised them (was there a word
For love in this wry tongue, or did they say
All things with similar lack of emphasis?)
But still the skies stayed friendly, even if
They found themselves being shouted at like deaf
-Mutes whom one naturally hates the more for this.

But that, too, passed. Their children now less often
Came red-eyed home from school.
                              Dour neighbours bent
Slowly like hazel twigs towards that sound,
Guttural, labial, but beginning to soften,
In which both earth and water were being blent
As it pulsed up in rich wells from underground.

BRUCE   DAWE

## Fairy Stories

But there were giants in the old days, men
with flaring nostrils and great yellow fangs
who made the mountains grumble with their pangs
of love or hunger. Legend has it, when

they howled at night they made the lightning fall
and sparks burst from their eyeballs. Later tribes
puzzled upon these histories of their scribes
and spat on their own flesh for being small.

And in the caves their poets would berate
loss of their shaggy innocence, and yearn
for the impossible ages to return,

while prophets cried how all the omens meant
some fabulous new vision lay in wait,
and how the future must be different.

CRAIG   POWELL

## Europe

The spy bears his bald intent like a manic
rattle through the street. A bitter rain
stains the cobblestones. A clock stops; elsewhere
winter tightens up its creaking grip.
Why does the soldier pace the empty field?
Whose war is this, so grey and easily spent?
Slow cars patrol the autoway, children
stare at you cruelly from behind an iron gate

and a brutish gathering begins, somewhere
on the plains far in the hinterland.
The black clock has been still for a hundred years,
and no peasant bears the luck to win
in this poor lottery. Dull green trucks roll out
and the countryside is well advised to be empty.

JOHN   TRANTER

# Villanelles

Among the metrical forms there are many patterns which are so restrictive that it is difficult to be more than just clever or fanciful within their limits. But there is one tightly controlled form, the villanelle, in which considerable achievement is possible. Originally French, it enjoyed a fashion in England about a century ago and has been tempting poets to try their skill ever since. Two lines in a villanelle are repeated separately throughout the poem and come together in the last stanza. Every line ends with one of two rhyme-sounds in the pattern aba, aba, aba, aba, aba, abab.

It's surprising how many different themes the poets have cast into this form. Les Murray's 'Commercial Hotel' is a good villanelle on an unexpected subject, and Nicholas Hasluck's (not so good: that 'peach' gets in only for the rhyme) is, even more surprisingly, a light-hearted comment on a news item. It was published in the *Australian* in January 1980.

Where the repeated lines can vary in their significance, like musical phrases repeated by different instruments, the villanelle can develop great power. Dylan Thomas's 'Do not go gentle into that good night' is a splendid example. In the first line he controls the speed by using not the adverb 'gently' which would make the line flow too smoothly, but the adjective 'gentle' which needs weightier utterance, almost as if there were commas before and after. Then 'that good night' (no hyphen) is veiled at first. We have to work towards the clear idea of death in later repeats, and so too with 'the dying of the light' in the other repeated line. The theme of the whole poem is contained in these two lines, but their full resonance is not achieved until the last defiant crescendo:

> Do not go gentle into that good night.
> Rage, rage against the dying of the light.

## Theocritus

O singer of Persephone!
    In the dim meadows desolate
Dost thou remember Sicily?

Still through the ivy flits the bee
    Where Amaryllis lies in state;
O Singer of Persephone!

Simaetha calls on Hecate
    And hears the wild dogs at the gate:
Dost thou remember Sicily?

Still by the light and laughing sea
    Poor Polypheme bemoans his fate;
O Singer of Persephone!

And still in boyish rivalry
    Young Daphnis challenges his mate;
Dost thou remember Sicily?

Slim Lacon keeps a goat for thee,
    For thee the jocund shepherds wait;
O Singer of Persephone!
Dost thou remember Sicily?

OSCAR WILDE

## If I Could Tell You

Time will say nothing but I told you so,
Time only knows the price we have to pay;
If I could tell you I would let you know.

If we should weep when clowns put on their show,
If we should stumble when musicians play,
Time will say nothing but I told you so.

There are no fortunes to be told, although,
Because I love you more than I can say,
If I could tell you I would let you know.

The winds must come from somewhere when they blow,
There must be reasons why the leaves decay;
Time will say nothing but I told you so.

Perhaps the roses really want to grow.
The vision seriously intends to stay;
If I could tell you I would let you know.

Suppose the lions all get up and go,
And all the brooks and soldiers run away;
Will Time say nothing but I told you so?
If I could tell you I would let you know.

W.H. AUDEN

## Missing Dates

Slowly the poison the whole blood stream fills.
It is not the effort nor the failure tires.
The waste remains, the waste remains and kills.

It is not your system or clear sight that mills
Down small to the consequence a life requires;
Slowly the poison the whole blood stream fills.

They bled an old dog dry yet the exchange rills
Of young dog blood gave but a month's desires.
The waste remains, the waste remains and kills.

It is the Chinese tombs and the slag hills
Usurp the soil, and not the soil retires.
Slowly the poison the whole blood stream fills.

Not to have fire is to be a skin that shrills.
The complete fire is death. From partial fires
The waste remains, the waste remains and kills.

It is the poems you have lost, the ills
From missing dates, at which the heart expires.
Slowly the poison the whole blood stream fills.
The waste remains, the waste remains and kills.

WILLIAM  EMPSON

## Do Not Go Gentle into That Good Night

Do not go gentle into that good night,
Old age should burn and rave at close of day;
Rage, rage against the dying of the light.

Though wise men at their end know dark is right,
Because their words had forked no lightning they
Do not go gentle into that good night.

Good men, the last wave by, crying how bright
Their frail deeds might have danced in a green bay,
Rage, rage against the dying of the light.

Wild men who caught and sang the sun in flight,
And learn, too late, they grieved it on its way,
Do not go gentle into that good night.

Grave men, near death, who see with blinding sight
Blind eyes could blaze like meteors and be gay,
Rage, rage against the dying of the light.

And you, my father, there on the sad height,
Curse, bless, me now with your fierce tears, I pray.
Do not go gentle into that good night.
Rage, rage against the dying of the light.

DYLAN   THOMAS

## The Commercial Hotel

Days of asphalt-blue and gold
murmurous with stout and flies,
lorries bought, allotments sold,

and recent heroes, newly old,
stare at their beer with bloating eyes.
Days of asphalt-blue and gold

dim to saloon bars, where unfold
subtleties of enterprise,
lorries bought, allotments sold,

where, with fingers burnt, the bold
learn to be indirect, and wise.
Days of asphalt-blue and gold

confirm the nation in its mould
of wages, contract and supplies,
lorries bought, allotments sold,

and the brave, their stories told,
age and regard, without surmise,
days of asphalt-blue and gold
lorries bought, allotments sold.

LES A. MURRAY

## The Words are There
*for Bruce Beaver*

There is a time and language to renew
so why curse all the moments when you're dumb?
The words are there, and have their work to do.

A man alone on a beach could find a clue,
proclaim what he and the ocean must become:
there is a time and language to renew

and cities to make whole. We muttering few
are strangers to all men and fools to some,
but words are there, and have their work to do.

Listen. I say that I could take you through
a street where blind men fester in a slum.
There is a time and language to renew.

But you know this far better than I do.
Then give speech to the speechless, nerves to the numb!
The words are there, and have their work to do.

Their song will be precise, the way that you
control the fury underneath your thumb.
There is a time and language to renew.
Your words are there, and have their work to do.

CRAIG POWELL

## Test Cricket

Twenty-four cans is the limit each!
The MCG laid down the law.
'What we know we have to teach.

Each esky must contain a peach,
a horseshoe roll and twenty-four.
Twenty-four cans is the limit each.'

Thirty-six would raise a screech.
Excessive drinking we all deplore.
What we know we have to teach.

A dozen stubbies can fill the breach
from three o'clock to half past four.
Twenty-four cans is the limit each.

A quiet ale within our reach.
That's all we ask. Nothing more.
What we know we have to teach.

Our dream is of an endless beach,
transistors murmuring the score.
What we know we have to teach.
Twenty-four cans is the limit each.

NICHOLAS   HASLUCK

# Odes

Odes come in all shapes and sizes, so it is impossible to provide a definition that will fit every known example. Essentially it is a sustained lyric on a noble or important subject, taking the form of an address to a person, object or personified power, and employing an elevated diction. Keats's 'Ode on a Grecian Urn', which is a grave meditation on the contrast between the timeless world of art and the fleeting world of man, begins with a formal address to the personified urn, seen in human terms as a 'bride of quietness' and a 'foster-child' of slow time. In Keats's 'Ode to a Nightingale', the formal address does not begin until the fifth line and only gradually is the nightingale transformed from a particular bird that 'singest of summer in full-throated ease' to a personification of something immortal in the universe: 'Thou wast not born for death, immortal Bird!' The concrete sensuous imagery throughout the poem creates a palpable identity between poet and bird and prevents the later personification from becoming vague or abstract.

Although both of Keats's Romantic Odes, like Shelley's 'Ode to the West Wind' are personal in many ways, they express general truths about life that have permanent validity. The choice of an ancient Greek urn as the main subject of one and the images of the 'emperor' and the Biblical Ruth in the other serve to create a sense of timelessness and universality through their references to the past. Life, it is suggested, has always been like this. And this generalising process is reinforced by the elevated tone and rather formal diction. Altogether simpler in form as befits its subject is Pope's 'Ode on Solitude'. Here there are no elaborate personifications, but instead an address to the ideal Happy Man and an enumeration of the pleasures that go to make up his happiness, each one expressed in simple memorable words. Such classic simplicity is typical of Pope's model, the Roman poet Horace who was the greatest writer of odes in Latin.

But odes need not always be serious. In his 'Ode on the Death of a Favourite Cat', the eighteenth-century poet Gray, who was one of the greatest writers of serious odes, writes a playful poem in which he uses the elevated tone and language proper to the ode to describe a trivial episode. Yet we notice that in the conclusion he preserves the convention of solemn moral reflection on life, but he does so ironically in a manner that is not entirely serious.

Odes are a great test of a poet's maturity of vision and verse technique. But one need not be a great poet to write a comic ode. Why not try it?

### Ode on Solitude

Happy the man, whose wish and care
A few paternal acres bound,
Content to breathe his native air
    In his own ground.

Whose herds with milk, whose fields with bread,
Whose flocks supply him with attire;
Whose trees in summer yield him shade,
    In winter fire.

Blest, who can unconcern'dly find
Hours, days, and years slide soft away
In health of body, peace of mind,
    Quiet by day,

Sound sleep by night; study and ease
Together mix'd; sweet recreation,
And innocence, which most does please
    With meditation.

Thus let me live, unseen, unknown;
Thus unlamented let me die;
Steal from the world, and not a stone
    Tell where I lie.

ALEXANDER  POPE

## Ode to a Nightingale

### I

My heart aches, and a drowsy numbness pains
  My sense, as though of hemlock I had drunk,
Or emptied some dull opiate to the drains
  One minute past, and Lethe-wards had sunk:
'Tis not through envy of thy happy lot,
    But being too happy in thine happiness,—
      That thou, light-winged Dryad of the trees,
        In some melodious plot
  Of beechen green, and shadows numberless,
    Singest of summer in full-throated ease.

### II

O, for a draught of vintage! that hath been
  Cooled a long age in the deep-delvèd earth,
Tasting of Flora and the country green,
  Dance, and Provençal song, and sunburnt mirth!
O for a beaker full of the warm South,
    Full of the true, the blushful Hippocrene,
      With beaded bubbles winking at the brim,
        And purple-stainèd mouth;
  That I might drink, and leave the world unseen,
    And with thee fade away into the forest dim:

### III

Fade far away, dissolve, and quite forget
  What thou among the leaves hast never known,
The weariness, the fever, and the fret
  Here, where men sit and hear each other groan;
Where palsy shakes a few, sad, last gray hairs,
    Where youth grows pale, and spectre-thin, and dies;
      Where but to think is to be full of sorrow
        And leaden-eyed despairs,
  Where Beauty cannot keep her lustrous eyes,
    Or new Love pine at them beyond to-morrow.

### IV

Away! away! for I will fly to thee,
  Not charioted by Bacchus and his pards,
But on the viewless wings of Poesy,
  Though the dull brain perplexes and retards:
Already with thee! tender is the night,
    And haply the Queen-Moon is on her throne,
      Clustered around by all her starry Fays;
        But here there is no light,
  Save what from heaven is with the breezes blown
    Through verdurous glooms and winding mossy ways.

V

I cannot see what flowers are at my feet,
   Nor what soft incense hangs upon the boughs,
But, in embalmèd darkness, guess each sweet
    Wherewith the seasonable month endows
The grass, the thicket, and the fruit-tree wild;
   White hawthorn, and the pastoral eglantine;
    Fast fading violets covered up in leaves;
      And mid-May's eldest child,
The coming musk-rose, full of dewy wine,
    The murmurous haunt of flies on summer eves.

VI

Darkling I listen; and, for many a time
   I have been half in love with easeful Death,
Called him soft names in many a musèd rhyme,
   To take into the air my quiet breath;
Now more than ever seems it rich to die,
   To cease upon the midnight with no pain,
    While thou art pouring forth thy soul abroad
      In such an ecstasy!
Still wouldst thou sing, and I have ears in vain—
   To thy high requiem become a sod.

VII

Thou was not born for death, immortal Bird!
   No hungry generations tread thee down;
The voice I hear this passing night was heard
   In ancient days by emperor and clown:
Perhaps the self-same song that found a path
   Through the sad heart of Ruth, when, sick for home,
    She stood in tears amid the alien corn;
      The same that oft-times hath
Charmed magic casements, opening on the foam
   Of perilous seas, in faery lands forlorn.

VIII

Forlorn! the very word is like a bell
   To toll me back from thee to my sole self!
Adieu! the fancy cannot cheat so well
   As she is famed to do, deceiving elf.
Adieu! adieu! thy plaintive anthem fades
   Past the near meadows, over the still stream,
    Up the hill-side; and now 'tis buried deep
      In the next valley-glades:
Was it a vision, or a waking dream?
   Fled is that music:—Do I wake or sleep?

JOHN KEATS

## Ode on a Grecian Urn

I

Thou still unravished bride of quietness,
   Thou foster-child of silence and slow time,
Sylvan historian, who canst thus express
   A flowery tale more sweetly than our rhyme:
What leaf-fringed legend haunts about thy shape
   Of deities or mortals, or of both,
      In Tempe or the dales of Arcady?
   What men or gods are these? What maidens loth?
What mad pursuit? What struggle to escape?
      What pipes and timbrels? What wild ecstasy?


II

Heard melodies are sweet, but those unheard
   Are sweeter; therefore, ye soft pipes, play on;
Not to the sensual ear, but, more endeared,
   Pipe to the spirit ditties of no tone:
Fair youth, beneath the trees, thou canst not leave
   Thy song, nor ever can those trees be bare;
      Bold Lover, never, never canst thou kiss,
Though winning near the goal—yet, do not grieve;
   She cannot fade, though thou hast not thy bliss,
      For ever wilt thou love, and she be fair!


III

Ah, happy, happy boughs! that cannot shed
   Your leaves, nor ever bid the Spring adieu;
And, happy melodist, unwearièd,
   For ever piping songs for ever new;
More happy love! more happy, happy love!
   For ever warm and still to be enjoyed,
      For ever panting, and for ever young;
All breathing human passion far above,
   That leaves a heart high-sorrowful and cloyed,
      A burning forehead, and a parching tongue.


IV

Who are these coming to the sacrifice?
   To what green altar, O mysterious priest,
Lead'st thou that heifer lowing at the skies,
   And all her silken flanks with garlands drest?
What little town by river or sea shore,
   Or mountain-built with peaceful citadel,
      Is emptied of this folk, this pious morn?
And, little town, thy streets for evermore
   Will silent be; and not a soul to tell
      Why thou art desolate, can e'er return.

V

O Attic shape! Fair attitude! with brede
  Of marble men and maidens overwrought,
With forest branches and the trodden weed;
  Thou, silent form, dost tease us out of thought
As doth eternity: Cold Pastoral!
  When old age shall this generation waste,
    Thou shalt remain, in midst of other woe
Than ours, a friend to man, to whom thou say'st,
  'Beauty is truth, truth beauty,' — that is all
    Ye know on earth, and all ye need to know.

JOHN KEATS

## Ode to the West Wind

I

O Wild West Wind, thou breath of Autumn's being,
  Thou, from whose unseen presence the leaves dead
Are driven, like ghosts from an enchanter fleeing,

  Yellow, and black, and pale, and hectic red,
Pestilence-stricken multitudes: O thou,
  Who chariotest to their dark wintry bed

The wingèd seeds, where they lie cold and low,
  Each like a corpse within its grave, until
Thine azure sister of the Spring shall blow

  Her clarion o'er the dreaming earth, and fill
(Driving sweet buds like flocks to feed in air)
  With living hues and odours plain and hill:

Wild Spirit, which art moving everywhere;
Destroyer and preserver; hear, O, hear!

II

Thou on whose stream, 'mid the steep sky's commotion,
  Loose clouds like earth's decaying leaves are shed,
Shook from the tangled boughs of Heaven and Ocean,

  Angels of rain and lightning: there are spread
On the blue surface of thine airy surge,
  Like the bright hair uplifted from the head

Of some fierce Maenad, even from the dim verge
  Of the horizon to the zenith's height,
The locks of the approaching storm. Thou dirge

Of the dying year, to which this closing night
Will be the dome of a vast sepulchre,
   Vaulted with all thy congregated might

Of vapours, from whose solid atmosphere
Black rain, and fire, and hail, will burst: O, hear!

III

Thou who didst waken from his summer dreams
   The blue Mediterranean, where he lay,
Lulled by the coil of his crystálline streams,

   Beside a pumice isle in Baiae's bay,
And saw in sleep old palaces and towers
   Quivering within the wave's intenser day,

All overgrown with azure moss, and flowers
   So sweet, the sense faints picturing them! Thou
For whose path the Atlantic's level powers

   Cleave themselves into chasms, while far below
The sea-blooms and the oozy woods which wear
   The sapless foliage of the ocean, know

Thy voice, and suddenly grow gray with fear,
And tremble and despoil themselves: O, hear!

IV

If I were a dead leaf thou mightest bear;
   If I were a swift cloud to fly with thee;
A wave to pant beneath thy power, and share

   The impulse of thy strength, only less free
Than thou, O uncontrollable! If even
   I were as in my boyhood, and could be

The comrade of thy wanderings over Heaven,
   As then, when to outstrip thy skiey speed
Scarce seemed a vision; I would ne'er have striven

   As thus with thee in prayer in my sore need.
Oh! lift me as a wave, a leaf, a cloud!
   I fall upon the thorns of life! I bleed!

A heavy weight of hours has chained and bowed
One too like thee: tameless, and swift, and proud.

V

Make me thy lyre, even as the forest is:
   What if my leaves are falling like its own!
The tumult of thy mighty harmonies

Will take from both a deep, autumnal tone,
Sweet though in sadness. Be thou, Spirit fierce,
   My spirit! Be thou me, impetuous one!

Drive my dead thoughts over the universe
   Like withered leaves, to quicken a new birth!
And, by the incantation of this verse,

   Scatter, as from an unextinguished hearth
Ashes and sparks, my words among mankind!
   Be through my lips to unawakened earth

The trumpet of a prophecy! O, Wind,
If Winter comes, can Spring be far behind?

PERCY BYSSHE SHELLEY

## Ode on the Death of a Favourite Cat

'Twas on a lofty vase's side,
Where China's gayest art had dyed
   The azure flowers, that blow;
Demurest of the tabby kind,
The pensive Selima reclined,
   Gazed on the lake below.

Her conscious tail her joy declared;
The fair round face, the snowy beard,
   The velvet of her paws,
Her coat, that with the tortoise vies,
Her ears of jet, and emerald eyes,
   She saw; and purred applause.

Still had she gazed; but 'midst the tide
Two angel forms were seen to glide,
   The genii of the stream;
Their scaly armour's Tyrian hue
Thro' richest purple to the view
   Betrayed a golden gleam.

The hapless nymph with wonder saw:
A whisker first, and then a claw,
   With many an ardent wish,
She stretched in vain to reach the prize.
What female heart can gold despise?
   What cat's averse to fish?

Presumptuous maid! with looks intent
Again she stretched, again she bent,
Nor knew the gulf between.
(Malignant Fate sat by and smiled)
The slippery verge her feet beguiled.
She tumbled headlong in.

Eight times emerging from the flood.
She mewed to every watery god,
Some speedy aid to send.
No dolphin came, no nereid stirred;
Nor cruel Tom, nor Susan heard.
A favourite has no friend!

From hence, ye beauties, undeceived,
Know one false step is ne'er retrieved,
And be with caution bold.
Not all that tempts your wandering eyes
And heedless hearts, is lawful prize,
Nor all that glisters, gold.

THOMAS   GRAY

# Elegiac Verse

Most of us at some time have suffered a desolate sense of loss. This may have been caused by a death or by the feeling that a moment of joy has gone for ever and can never be recaptured. In such a mood we long for some consolation that will reconcile us to our sense of loss and thus make the death or lost happiness more bearable. The kind of poem that focuses on this pattern of loss and reconciliation is the elegy. In English as distinct from Latin poetry, there is no special metre or system of versification for writing elegies. Indeed, the poems in this section show what a variety of forms the elegy may take, from Gray's long formal 'Elegy Written in a Country Churchyard' to James McAuley's brief poem, 'Pieta', in which the Catholic poet finds religious consolation for the loss of his new-born child.

For an unbeliever like Hardy no such consolation is available. In the poems he wrote in 1912-13 on his early happiness with his first wife Emma (of which 'After a Journey' is an example), he becomes reconciled to her death and his lost happiness by recreating the past with such dramatic immediacy that it establishes the integrity and survival of their relationship beyond death. For the Australian poet, John Manifold, the consolation for the death of his soldier friend Lt John Learmonth comes from two sources. It comes from the self-delighting act of poetic creation itself:

> This is not sorrow, this is work: I build
> A cairn of words over a silent man.

It also comes from the recognition of the dead man's simple heroism. Thus he concludes his elegy:

> Let others mourn and feel
> He died for nothing: nothings have their place.
> While thus the kind and civilised conceal

This spring of unsuspected inward grace
And look on death as equals, I am filled
With queer affection for the human race.

It is one of the paradoxes of the pattern of poetry called an elegy that, although it celebrates death and sorrow, its final effect is often tonic and bracing rather than depressing.

Howard Sergeant's 'The Inarticulate' and the Australian migrant poet Peter Skrzynecki's 'Elegy for Don McLaughlin' are useful reminders that elegies can celebrate the meaning of death and loss in ordinary life and are not reserved for heroic people or great events. As in so many elegies since Hardy, the consolation in Peter Skrzynecki's poem about death in a car crash springs from the intensity with which the poet identifies himself with his dead school friend, Don McLaughlin. The imagery builds up a vivid impression of the suburban life he shared with the dead boy. In many of the other elegies in this section the imagery has a generalising function, linking the sense of individual loss to the sadness at the heart of things, as in 'Fidele's Dirge' from Shakespeare's play *Cymbeline,* or to the whole cosmic process, as in Tennyson's 'Break, break, break' or in Wordsworth's 'A Slumber did my Spirit Seal':

No motion has she now, no force;
   She neither hears nor sees;
Rolled round in earth's diurnal course,
   With rocks, and stones, and trees.

### The Coat

After years in a storage suitcase
it gets its first post-mortem airing: my
father's gaberdine coat, one of the relics
given me when he died. Shoving my fists
deep in the pockets, I touch shreds of tobacco.

For forty years he rolled his own. Always he
would be smoking. And that day when his heart
gave its last cough, they found him on the floor
with a bent cigarette beside his face.
Later I saw him disappear
through curtains of the crematorium
to smoke.

I have my hands in his pockets
and in my hands his brittle remains.

IAN REID

## The Inarticulate

His name was never mentioned in despatches,
Nor was he hero of the desperate stand.
His death obscured no headlines, roused no snatches
Of sympathy or personal sense of loss
Even in comrade hearts. Under strict command
Of parent, schoolmaster, and caustic boss,
His mind and limbs were harnessed to the clock;
And all his hours were blossoms for others to tread.
He gathered experience from the books he read,
And clambered mountains with a dreamer's alpenstock.
From attic windows he watched the white rains falling
But lacked the sounding-thought to fathom flood.
His was the voice of the lonely seagull calling
Over the rooftops to winds and an empty sky.
He sought no revelation in unfolding bud;
Nor claimed a nobler cause for which to die
Than the accidental bursting of a gun:
So little song or colour to warrant his remaining—
Yet one there was for whom his life held meaning,
And with his passing, grief walled up the sun.

HOWARD   SERGEANT

## Pietà

A year ago you came
Early into the light.
You lived a day and night,
Then died; no one to blame.

Once only, with one hand,
Your mother in farewell
Touched you. I cannot tell,
I cannot understand

A thing so dark and deep,
So physical a loss:
One touch, and that was all

She had of you to keep.
Clean wounds, but terrible,
Are those made with the Cross.

JAMES   MCAULEY

## After a Journey

Hereto I come to view a voiceless ghost;
   Whither, O whither will its whim now draw me?
Up the cliff, down, till I'm lonely, lost,
   And the unseen waters' ejaculations awe me.
Where you will next be there's no knowing,
    Facing round about me everywhere,
      With your nut-coloured hair,
And gray eyes, and rose-flush coming and going.

Yes: I have re-entered your olden haunts at last;
   Through the years, through the dead scenes I have tracked you;

What have you now found to say of our past—
   Scanned across the dark space wherein I have lacked you?
Summer gave us sweets, but autumn wrought division?
    Things were not lastly as firstly well
      With us twain, you tell?
But all's closed now, despite Time's derision.

I see what you are doing: you are leading me on
   To the spots we knew when we haunted here together,
The waterfall, above which the mist-bow shone
   At the then fair hour in the then fair weather,
And the cave just under, with a voice still so hollow
    That it seems to call out to me from forty years ago,
      When you were all aglow,
And not the thin ghost that I now frailly follow!

Ignorant of what there is flitting here to see,
   The waked birds preen and the seals flop lazily;
Soon you will have, Dear, to vanish from me,
   For the stars close their shutters and the dawn whitens hazily.
Trust me, I mind not, though Life lours,
   The bringing me here; nay, bring me here again!
    I am just the same as when
Our days were a joy, and our paths through flowers.

THOMAS  HARDY

## Elegy for Don McLaughlin

An only child also
You were equally spoilt—
Taken to both extremes,
Paradise and Inferno;
While parents kept guard
With upraised hands
Against vices and year-round chills.

Your voice
A good-luck charm
You sang like Burns wrote poetry—
Purely, the accent on love;
At concerts and plays
It drew admiration
As death draws silence.

We raced each other
To school in the mornings;
Beginning at opposite ends of the hill
On which St Peter's stands,
Swerving and skiting
On our bikes—unafraid
Of cars or Sister Brendan's cautions,
Laughing, out of breath.
Two fifth grade heroes
Chastized before the class—
Called 'bold, brazen lads'
For the *n*th time.

On Berala station
They told me how you died—
With all the 'ifs' and 'buts'
That make Fate
So ominuous and unkind:
A stolen car, the head-on smash,
You the only one
Not to survive.
A girl in a yellow dress
Held a transistor
To the wind:
                    the Stones
Thumped out *The Last Time*
As our train
Came noisily in.

I wondered
How dark the night had been,
If any song
Had come to mind?

In those morning runs
You always beat me up the hill.
Younger by two years
I was fifteen when you died—
Old enough for self-esteem
And showing I wouldn't cry.
Now, on the same road,
I catch up to you
Without even having to try.

PETER   SKRZYNECKI

### The Boy

By God grieve for the boy lost or broken
Who lived in books and mountain bush, both loved.
Dreaming and free, he breathed the words and wind,
Enacting in trees the scenes the books had spoken
And, in stories, however far removed,
Some of the soul of his own father land.

Now lost or dead, by mankind overtaken
Or by the mountains of men overgrown,
He lies among green brambles in the tomb,
In the words of a world more than wind-shaken,
And in the man he has become, alone.
Dreamless and bound, he is no longer home.

But grieving him, go in search with wonder
To know all that he loved and vanished under.

DAVID  CAMPBELL

### Dead Boy

The little cousin is dead, by foul subtraction,
A green bough from Virginia's aged tree,
And none of the county kin like the transaction,
Nor some of the world of outer dark, like me.

A boy not beautiful, nor good, nor clever,
A black cloud full of storms too hot for keeping,
A sword beneath his mother's heart—yet never
Woman bewept her babe as this is weeping.

A pig with a pasty face, so I had said,
Squealing for cookies, kinned by poor pretense
With a noble house. But the little man quite dead,
I see the forbears' antique lineaments.

The elder men have strode by the box.of death
To the wide flag porch, and muttering low send round
The bruit of the day. O friendly waste of breath!
Their hearts are hurt with a deep dynastic wound.

He was pale and little, the foolish neighbors say;
The first-fruits saith the Preacher, the Lord hath taken;
But this was the old tree's late branch wrenched away,
Grieving the sapless limbs, the shorn and shaken.

JOHN  CROWE  RANSOM

## Three Weeks Ago

Three weeks ago
they weeded the family grave,
made a tentative booking with a funeral firm,
came home to watch her die.

Feet first against the dark;
speech, hearing, sight
shut down far under the surface of flesh.
They urged her on with frequent visits,
read the bible like a tourist brochure,
engaged an official guide.

She gave in at last,
went without saying goodbye.
Her room is resting from the strain;
sits alone quietly
with a cup of tea.

CHRISTINE CHURCHES

## The Choice

I have known one bound to a bed by wrist and ankle
Scarred by the whips of a wasting ache
Who at the point of entering of the needle
Looked once around to take
The final view, then spoke:
The echo of that terribly witty joke
Pursued the surgeon to his home in Kew,
Deafened a nurse all night and leaden lay
On the heart of a thick-skinned anaesthetist
Long after they'd dispatched his ended clay.

*That one lies in Oxford and is its earth.*
Also a bright-eyed woman in Germany
In a sightless trap far below ground
Of which another held the key
Surveyed without visible alarm
Or twitch of pinioned arm
The instruments set out upon a table:
Then from her mouth there flowed a resolute
Stream of satire deliciously edged until
Then tormentor tormented stopped it with a boot.

*She fell as ash not bones in Herzen fields:*
*All brave men breathe her when the wind*
*Blows east from Danube.* And Tom Caine

When the 'Imperial' was mined
And water had flooded all but the wireless-room
Spoke without audible gloom
From fifty fathoms down for fifteen hours
To his mess-mates on land, told several stories,
Then to a doctor carefully descibed
Asphyxiation's onset and his doom.

*He is grown water and surrounds the pole:*
*If ever you dip a cup in any sea*
*Tom Caine is in it somewhere.* On the whole
Men die asleep or else disgracefully;
But not all men. Perhaps we are never
By any average mountain wood or river
More than a heart's-breadth from the dust
Of one who laughed with nothing left to lose.
Who saw the joke beneath the mammoth's foot?
And what shall I choose, if I am free to choose?

HILARY CORKE

## The Tomb of Lt John Learmonth, A.I.F.

'At the end on Crete he took to the hills, and said he'd fight it
out with only a revolver. He was a great soldier.' . . .
*—One of his men in a letter.*

This is not sorrow, this is work: I build
A cairn of words over a silent man,
My friend John Learmonth whom the Germans killed.

There was no word of hero in his plan;
Verse should have been his love and peace his trade,
But history turned him to a partisan.

Far from the battle as his bones are laid
Crete will remember him. Remember well,
Mountains of Crete, the Second Field Brigade!

Say Crete, and there is little more to tell
Of muddle tall as treachery, despair
And black deafeat resounding like a bell;

But bring the magnifying focus near
And in contempt of muddle and defeat
The old heroic virtues still appear.

Australian blood where hot and icy meet
(James Hogg and Lermontov were of his kin)
Lie still and fertilise the fields of Crete.

*

Schoolboy, I watched his ballading begin:
Billy and bullocky and billabong,
Our properties of childhood, all were in.

I heard the air though not the undersong,
The fierceness and resolve; but all the same
They're the tradition, and tradition's strong.

Swagman and bushranger die hard, die game,
Die fighting, like that wild colonial boy —
Jack Dowling, says the ballad, was his name.

He also spun his pistol like a toy,
Turned to the hills like wolf or kangaroo,
And faced destruction with a bitter joy.

His freedom gave him nothing else to do
But set his back against his family tree
And fight the better for the fact he knew

He was as good as dead. Because the sea
Was closed and the air dark and the land lost,
'They'll never capture me alive,' said he.

                              *


That's courage chemically pure, uncrossed
With sacrifice or duty or career,
Which counts and pays in ready coin the cost

Of holding course. Armies are not its sphere
Where all's contrived to achieve its counterfeit;
It swears with discipline, it's volunteer.

I could as hardly make a moral fit
Around it as around a lightning flash.
There is no moral, that's the point of it,

No moral. But I'm glad of this panache
That sparkles, as from flint, from us and steel,
True to no crown nor presidential sash

Nor flag nor fame. Let others mourn and feel
He died for nothing: nothings have their place.
While thus the kind and civilised conceal

This spring of unsuspected inward grace
And look on death as equals, I am filled
With queer affection for the human race.

                              JOHN   MANIFOLD

## Beach Burial

Softly and humbly to the Gulf of Arabs
The convoys of dead sailors come;
At night they away and wander in the waters far under,
But morning rolls them in the foam.

Between the sob and clubbing of the gunfire
Someone, it seems, has time for this,
To pluck them from the shallows and bury them in burrows
And tread the sand upon their nakedness;

And each cross, the driven stake of tidewood,
Bears the last signature of men,
Written with such perplexity, with such bewildered pity,
The words choke as they begin —

*'Unknown seaman'*—the ghostly pencil
Wavers and fades, the purple drips,
The breath of the wet season has washed their inscriptions
As blue as drowned men's lips,

Dead seamen, gone in search of the same landfall,
Whether as enemies they fought,
Or fought with us, or neither; the sand joins them together,
Enlisted on the other front.

*El Alamein*

KENNETH   SLESSOR

## In Flanders Fields

In Flanders fields the poppies blow
Between the crosses, row on row
　　That mark our place; and in the sky
　　The larks, still bravely singing, fly
Scarce heard amid the guns below.

We are the Dead. Short days ago
We lived, felt dawn, saw sunset glow,
　　Loved and were loved, and now we lie
　　　　In Flanders fields.

Take up our quarrel with the foe:
To you from failing hands we throw
　　The torch; be yours to hold it high.
　　If ye break faith with us who die
We shall not sleep, though poppies grow
　　　　In Flanders fields.

JOHN   McCREA

## Elegy Written in a Country Churchyard

The curfew tolls the knell of parting day,
  The lowing herd wind slowly o'er the lea,
The ploughman homeward plods his weary way,
  And leaves the world to darkness and to me.

Now fades the glimmering landscape on the sight,
  And all the air a solemn stillness holds,
Save where the beetle wheels his droning flight,
  And drowsy tinklings lull the distant folds;

Save that from yonder ivy-mantled tower
  The moping owl does to the moon complain
Of such, as wandering near her secret bower,
  Molest her ancient solitary reign.

Beneath those rugged elms, that yew-tree's shade,
  Where heaves the turf in many a mouldering heap,
Each in his narrow cell for ever laid,
  The rude forefathers of the hamlet sleep.

The breezy call of incense-breathing Morn,
  The swallow twittering from the straw-built shed,
The cock's shrill clarion, or the echoing horn,
  No more shall rouse them from their lowly bed.

For them no more the blazing hearth shall burn,
  Or busy housewife ply her evening care:
No children run to lisp their sire's return,
  Or climb his knees the envied kiss to share.

Oft did the harvest to their sickle yield,
  Their furrow oft the stubborn glebe has broke;
How jocund did they drive their team afield!
  How bowed the woods beneath their sturdy stroke!

Let not Ambition mock their useful toil,
  Their homely joys, and destiny obscure;
Nor Grandeur hear with a disdainful smile
  The short and simple annals of the poor.

The boast of heraldry, the pomp of power,
  And all that beauty, all that wealth e'er gave,
Awaits alike the inevitable hour:
  The paths of glory lead but to the grave.

Nor you, ye proud, impute to these the fault,
  If Memory o'er their tomb no trophies raise,
Where through the long-drawn aisle and fretted vault
  The pealing anthem swells the note of praise.

Can storied urn or animated bust
   Back to its mansion call the fleeting breath?
Can Honour's voice provoke the silent dust,
   Or Flattery soothe the dull cold ear of death?

Perhaps in this neglected spot is laid
   Some heart once pregnant with celestial fire;
Hands, that the rod of empire might have swayed,
   Or waked to ecstasy the living lyre.

But Knowledge to their eyes her ample page
   Rich with the spoils of time did ne'er unroll;
Chill Penury repressed their noble rage,
   And froze the genial current of the soul.

Full many a gem of purest ray serene
   The dark unfathomed caves of ocean bear:
Full many a flower is born to blush unseen,
   And waste its sweetness on the desert air.

Some village Hampden, that with dauntless breast
   The little tyrant of his fields withstood;
Some mute inglorious Milton here may rest,
   Some Cromwell, guiltless of his country's blood.

The applause of listening senates to command,
   The threats of pain and ruin to despise,
To scatter plenty o'er a smiling land,
   And read their history in a nation's eyes,

Their lot forbad: nor circumscribed alone
   Their growing virtues, but their crimes confined;
Forbad to wade through slaughter to a throne,
   And shut the gates of mercy on mankind;

The struggling pangs of conscious truth to hide,
   To quench the blushes of ingenuous shame,
Or heap the shrine of Luxury and Pride
   With incense kindled at the Muse's flame.

Far from the madding crowd's ignoble strife
   Their sober wishes never learned to stray;
Along the cool sequestered vale of life
   They kept the noiseless tenor of their way.

Yet even these bones from insult to protect
   Some frail memorial still erected nigh,
With uncouth rhymes and shapeless sculpture decked,
   Implores the passing tribute of a sigh.

Their name, their years, spelt by the unlettered Muse,
   The place of fame and elegy supply:
And many a holy text around she strews,
   That teach the rustic moralist to die.

For who, to dumb forgetfulness a prey,
   This pleasing anxious being e'er resigned,
Left the warm precincts of the cheerful day,
   Nor cast one longing lingering look behind?

On some fond breast the parting soul relies,
   Some pious drops the closing eye requires;
E'en from the tomb the voice of Nature cries,
   E'en in our ashes live their wonted fires.

For thee, who, mindful of the unhonoured dead,
   Dost in these lines their artless tale relate;
If chance, by lonely contemplation led,
   Some kindred spirit shall inquire thy fate,

Haply some hoary-headed swain may say,
   'Oft have we seen him at the peep of dawn
Brushing with hasty steps the dews away
   To meet the sun upon the upland lawn.

'There at the foot of yonder nodding beech
   That wreathes its old fantastic roots so high,
His listless length at noontide would he stretch,
   And pore upon the brook that babbles by.

'Hard by yon wood, now smiling as in scorn,
   Muttering his wayward fancies he would rove;
Now drooping, woeful wan, like one forlorn,
   Or crazed with care, or crossed in hopeless love.

'One morn I missed him on the customed hill,
   Along the heath and near his favourite tree;
Another came; nor yet beside the rill,
   Nor up the lawn, nor at the wood was he;

'The next with dirges due in sad array
   Slow through the church-way path we saw him borne;—
Approach and read (for thou canst read) the lay,
   Graved on the stone beneath yon aged thorn.'

THE EPITAPH
   *Here rests his head upon the lap of Earth,*
      *A youth, to Fortune and to Fame unknown:*
   *Fair Science frowned not on his humble birth,*
      *And Melancholy marked him for her own.*

*Large was his bounty, and his soul sincere,*
  *Heaven did a recompense as largely send:*
*He give to Misery all he had, a tear,*
  *He gained from Heaven ('twas all he wished) a friend.*

*No farther seek his merits to disclose,*
  *Or draw his frailties from their dread abode,*
*(There they alike in trembling hope repose,)*
  *The bosom of his Father and his God.*

THOMAS  GRAY

## In Plague Time

Adieu, farewell earth's bliss,
This world uncertain is;
Fond are life's lustful joys,
Death proves them all but toys,
None from his darts can fly.
I am sick, I must die.
    Lord, have mercy on us!

Rich men, trust not in wealth,
Gold cannot buy you health;
Physic himself must fade,
All things to end are made.
The plague full swift goes by.
I am sick, I must die.
    Lord, have mercy on us!

Beauty is but a flower
Which wrinkles will devour;
Brightness falls from the air,
Queens have died young and fair,
Dust hath closed Helen's eye.
I am sick, I must die.
    Lord, have mercy on us!

Strength stoops unto the grave,
Worms feed on Hector brave,
Swords may not fight with fate,
Earth still holds ope her gate.
Come! come! the bells do cry.
I am sick, I must die.
    Lord, have mercy on us!

Wit with his wantonness
Tasteth death's bitterness;
Hell's executioner
Hath no ears for to hear
What vain art can reply.
I am sick, I must die.
      Lord, have mercy on us!

Haste, therefore, each degree,
To welcome destiny.
Heaven is our heritage,
Earth but a player's stage;
Mount we unto the sky.
I am sick, I must die.
      Lord, have mercy on us!

THOMAS NASHE

## Fidele's Dirge

Fear no more the heat o' the sun,
  Nor the furious winter's rages;
Thou thy worldly task hast done,
   Home art gone, and ta'en thy wages.
Golden lads and girls all must,
As chimney-sweepers, come to dust.

Fear no more the frown o' the great,
   Thou art past the tyrant's stroke;
Care no more to clothe and eat,
   To thee the reed is as the oak.
The sceptre, learning, physic, must
All follow this, and come to dust.

Fear no more the lightning-flash,
   Nor the all-dreaded thunder-stone;
Fear not slander, censure rash;
   Thou hast finished joy and moan.
All lovers young, all lovers must
Consign to thee, and come to dust.

No exorciser harm thee!
Nor no witchcraft charm thee!
Ghost unlaid forbear thee!
Nothing ill come near thee!
Quiet consummation have,
And renowned be thy grave!

WILLIAM SHAKESPEARE

## Break, Break, Break

Break, break, break,
　On thy cold gray stones, O Sea!
And I would that my tongue could utter
　The thoughts that arise in me.

O well for the fisherman's boy,
　That he shouts with his sister at play!
O well for the sailor lad,
　That he sings in his boat on the bay!

And the stately ships go on
　To their haven under the hill;
But O for the touch of a vanished hand,
　And the sound of a voice that is still!

Break, break, break,
　At the foot of thy crags, O Sea!
But the tender grace of a day that is dead
　Will never come back to me.

ALFRED,　LORD TENNYSON

## A Slumber Did my Spirit Seal

A slumber did my spirit seal;
　I had no human fears:
She seemed a thing that could not feel
　The touch of earthly years.

No motion has she now, no force;
　She neither hears nor sees;
Rolled round in earth's diurnal course,
　With rocks, and stones, and trees.

WILLIAM　WORDSWORTH

## Elegy for Drowned Children

What does he do with them all, the old king:
Having such a shining haul of boys in his sure net,
How does he keep them happy, lead them to forget
The world above, the aching air, birds, spring?

Tender and solicitous must be his care
For these whom he takes down into his kingdom one by one
—Why else would they be taken out of the sweet sun,
Drowning towards him, water plaiting their hair?

Unless he loved them deeply how could he withstand
The voices of parents calling, calling like birds by the water's edge,
By swimming-pool, sand-bar, river-bank, rocky ledge,
The little heaps of clothes, the futures carefully planned?

Yet even an old acquisitive king must feel
Remorse poisoning his joy, since he allows
Particular boys each evening to arouse
From leaden-lidded sleep, softly to steal

Away to the whispering shore, there to plunge in,
And fluid as porpoises swim upward, upward through the dividing
Waters until, soon, each back home is striding
Over thresholds of welcome dream with wet and moonlit skin.

BRUCE   DAWE

### The Mill-Water

Only the sound remains
Of the old mill;
Gone is the wheel;
On the prone roof and walls the nettle reigns.

Water that toils no more
Dangles white locks
And, falling, mocks
The music of the mill-wheel's busy roar.

Pretty to see, by day
Its sound is naught
Compared with thought
And talk and noise of labour and of play.

Night makes the difference.
In calm moonlight,
Gloom infinite,
The sound comes surging in upon the sense:

Solitude, company,—
When it is night,—
Grief or delight
By it must haunted or concluded be.

Often the silentness
Has but this one
Companion;
Wherever one creeps in the other is:

Sometimes a thought is drowned
By it, sometimes
Out of it climbs;
All thoughts begin or end upon this sound,

Only the idle foam
Of water falling
Changelessly calling,
Where once men had a work-place and a home.

EDWARD   THOMAS

# Dramatic Verse

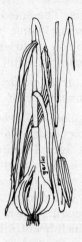

Some poems create a situation that reminds us of a scene from a play. We may call these dramatic poems. Often they contain characters other than the poet, as in Browning's dramatic monologue 'My Last Duchess', in which he creates the character of a great Renaissance nobleman who is negotiating with an envoy for a second marriage, having in the past ordered the death of his first wife, whose picture and character he describes to the silent listening envoy. The duke does all the talking. In some respects the dramatic monologue is like one of Shakespeare's soliloquies when a character is alone on the stage and speaks his inner thoughts so that the audience enters into his state of mind and feeling. In a similar fashion, because the character in a dramatic monologue also speaks his inner thought, we identify to some extent with him, however villainous he may be, and see the situation through his eyes; but, because the poet also creates the world around him as well, we see that the character's account of the situation is only one of the possible ones, and an imperfect one at that. The structure of the dramatic monologue and the ironically controlled voice of the speaker, therefore, enable us to judge the central character as well as enter his mind. Descriptive details in Browning's poem act as an implicit criticism of the Duke's worldliness, while his own speech is an example of judgment through self revelation, since as he speaks he reveals his insane family pride, his treatment of his first wife as just another costly 'possession', and his capricious cruelty. As a form, the dramatic monologue has appealed to modern poets since Browning, because it is an ideal form for suggesting that truth is to some extent relative and because it offers a way of criticising false values in a subtle and indirect manner.

The speaker in John Betjeman's 'In Westminster Abbey' is a silly self-regarding patriotic Christian who misapplies Christian principles in time of war and thus provides her own self-judgment. She stands condemned out of her own mouth. Because the poet deliberately exaggerates her attitude into a broad parody we find the poem amusing, but it has its serious side as well, since many readers will uncomfortably recognise some of their own sillier sentiments expressed in the speaker's words. The speaker in Betjeman's other dramatic monologue is a brash up-and-coming young executive who sees all life in terms of commercial success and snobbish luxuries. He is made to reveal his false values through the language he uses. It is full of such jargon as:

> Essentially I integrate the current export drive
> And basically I'm viable from ten o'clock till five.

Anyone who thinks in such language soon ceases to think at all. The imagery throughout, which is related to acquisition and material ownership, reinforces the point of the poem. Randall Jarrell makes a similar use of the dramatic monologue in a poem appropriately called 'Money'. In it the dramatised American speaker sums up his whole philosophy of life in the single line: 'I never saw a man I couldn't buy'. In complete contrast to this wealthy man's complacent materialism is the moving West Indian poem 'The Lament of the Banana Man' by Evan John, which beautifully captures the mixed feelings of the uprooted West Indian speaker through the exact lilt and idiom of the West Indian speech.

> Gal, I'm tellin' you, I'm tired fo' true,
> Tired of Englan', tired o' you.
> But I can't go back to Jamaica now . . .

Poems can be dramatic in many other ways, through conflict and confrontation, for example. Both are present in the Canadian poet Earl Birney's 'Meeting of Strangers'. There is a marvellous mixture of the sinister and the comic in this dramatic account of the poet's momentary and unexpected encounter with a potential mugger who takes a liking to his jacket, and we presume to the contents of its pockets. In Gwen Harwood's 'Barn Owl', the encounter is not with a person but with an owl, which the child shoots and in doing so destroys her innocence and enters an adult world of guilt and remorse. The contrasting images of sight and blindness, of innocence and experience, of peace and violence reinforce the sense of dramatic conflict. Since all life involves dramatic conflict of some kind, the poems in this section take us close to the heart of things.

### To Be, or Not to Be

> To be, or not to be—that is the question.
> Whether 'tis nobler in the mind to suffer
> The slings and arrows of outrageous fortune,
> Or to take arms against a sea of troubles,
> And by opposing end them?—To die—to sleep—
> No more; and by a sleep to say we end
> The heart-ache, and the thousand natural shocks

That flesh is heir to ; 'tis a consummation
Devoutly to be wished. To die—to sleep—
To sleep! perchance to dream. Ay, there's the rub;
For in that sleep of death what dreams may come,
When we have shuffled off this mortal coil,
Must give us pause. There's the respect
That makes calamity of so long life.
For who would bear the whips and scorns of time,
The oppressor's wrong, the proud man's contumely,
The pangs of despised love, the law's delay,
The insolence of office, and the spurns
That patient merit of the unworthy takes,
When he himself might his quietus make
With a bare bodkin? Who would fardels bear,
To grunt and sweat under a weary life,
But that the dread of something after death—
The undiscovered country from whose bourn
No traveller returns—puzzles the will,
And makes us rather bear those ills we have
Than fly to others that we know not of?
Thus conscience does make cowards of us all,
And thus the native hue of resolution
Is sicklied o'er with the pale cast of thought;
And enterprises of great pitch and moment,
With this regard, their currents turn awry,
And lose the name of action.

WILLIAM SHAKESPEARE

## Journey of the Magi

'A cold coming we had of it,
Just the worst time of the year
For a journey, and such a long journey:
The ways deep and the weather sharp,
The very dead of winter.'
And the camels galled, sore-footed, refractory,
Lying down in the melting snow.
There were times we regretted
The summer palaces on slopes, the terraces,
And the silken girls bringing sherbert.
Then the camel men cursing and grumbling
And running away, and wanting their liquor and women,
And the night-fires going out, and the lack of shelters,

And the cities hostile and the towns unfriendly
And the villages dirty and charging high prices:
A hard time we had of it.
At the end we preferred to travel all night,
Sleeping in snatches,
With the voices singing in our ears, saying
That this was all folly.

Then at dawn we came down to a temperate valley,
Wet, below the snow line, smelling of vegetation;
With a running stream and a water-mill beating the darkness,
And three trees on the low sky,
And an old white horse galloped away in the meadow.
Then we came to a tavern with vine-leaves over the lintel,
Six hands at an open door dicing for pieces of silver,
And feet kicking the empty wine-skins.
But there was no information, and so we continued
And arrived at evening, not a moment too soon
Finding the place; it was (you may say) satisfactory.

All this was a long time ago, I remember,
And I would do it again, but set down
This set down
This: were we led all that way for
Birth or Death? There was a Birth, certainly,
We had evidence and no doubt. I had seen birth and death,
But had thought they were different; this Birth was
Hard and bitter agony for us, like Death, our death.
We returned to our places, these Kingdoms,
But no longer at ease here, in the old dispensation,
With an alien people clutching their gods.
I should be glad of another death.

T.S. ELIOT

## My Last Duchess

That's my last Duchess painted on the wall,
Looking as if she were alive. I call
That piece a wonder, now: Frà Pandolf's hands
Worked busily a day, and there she stands.
Will 't please you sit and look at her? I said
'Fra Pandolf' by design, for never read

Strangers like you that pictured countenance,
The depth and passion of its earnest glance,
But to myself they turned (since none puts by
The curtain I have drawn for you, but I)
And seemed as they would ask me, if they durst,
How such a glance came there; so, not the first
Are you to turn and ask thus. Sir 'twas not
Her husband's presence only, called that spot
Of joy into the Duchess' cheek: perhaps
Frà Pandolf chanced to say, 'Her mantle laps
Over my lady's wrist too much,' or 'Paint
Must never hope to reproduce the faint
Half-flush that dies along her throat:' such stuff
Was courtesy, she thought, and cause enough
For calling up that spot of joy. She had
A heart—how shall I say?—too soon made glad,
Too easily impressed; she liked whate'er
She looked on, and her looks went everywhere.
Sir, 'twas all one! My favour at her breast,
The dropping of the daylight in the West,
The bough of cherries some officious fool
Broke in the orchard for her, the white mule
She rode with round the terrace—all and each
Would draw from her alike the approving speech,
Or blush, at least. She thanked men,—good! but thanked
Somehow—I know not how—as if she ranked
My gift of a nine-hundred-years-old name
With anybody's gift. Who'd stoop to blame
This sort of trifling? Even had you skill
In speech—(which I have not)—to make your will
Quite clear to such an one, and say, 'Just this
Or that in you disgusts me; here you miss,
Or there exceed the mark' — and if she let
Herself be lessoned so, nor plainly set
Her wits to yours, forsooth, and made excuse,
—E'en then would be some stooping; and I choose
Never to stoop. Oh sir, she smiled, no doubt,
Whene'er I passed her; but who passed without
Much the same smile? This grew; I gave commands;
Then all smiles stopped together. There she stands
As if alive. Will 't please you rise? We'll meet
The company below, then. I repeat,
The Count your master's known munificence
Is ample warrant that no just pretence
Of mine for dowry will be disallowed;
Though his fair daughter's self, as I avowed
At starting, is my object. Nay, we'll go
Together down, sir. Notice Neptune, though,
Taming a sea-horse, thought a rarity,
Which Claus of Innsbruck cast in bronze for me!

ROBERT  BROWNING

## Telephone Conversation

The price seemed reasonable, location
Indifferent. The landlady swore she lived
Off premises. Nothing remained
But self-confession. 'Madam,' I warned,
'I hate a wasted journey—I am—African.'
Silence. Silenced transmission of
Pressurised good-breeding. Voice, when it came,
Lip-stick coated, long gold-rolled
Cigarette-holder pipped. Caught I was, foully.
'HOW DARK?' ... I had not misheard ... 'ARE YOU LIGHT
OR VERY DARK?' Button B. Button A. Stench
Of rancid breath of public-hide-and-speak.
Red booth. Red pillar-box. Red double-tiered
Omnibus squelching tar. It *was* real! Shamed
By ill-mannered silence, surrender
Pushed dumbfoundment to beg simplification.
Considerate she was, varying the emphasis—
'ARE YOU DARK? OR VERY LIGHT?' Revelation came.
'You mean—like plain or milk chocolate?'
Her assent was clinical, crushing in its light
Impersonality. Rapidly, wave-length adjusted,
I chose, 'West African sepia'—and as an afterthought,
'Down in my passport.' Silence for spectroscopic
Flight of fancy, till truthfulness clanged her accent
Hard on the mouthpiece. 'WHAT'S THAT?' conceding
'DON'T KNOW WHAT THAT IS.' 'Like brunette.'
'THAT'S DARK, ISN'T IT?' 'Not altogether.
'Facially, I am brunette, but madam, you should see
The rest of me. Palm of my hand, soles of my feet
Are a peroxide blond. Friction, caused—
Foolishly madam—by sitting down, has turned
My bottom raven black—One moment madam!'—sensing
Her receiver rearing on the thunder clap
About my ears—'Madam,' I pleaded, 'Wouldn't you rather
See for yourself?'

WOLE  SOYINKA

## In Westminster Abbey

Let me take this other glove off
    As the *vox humana* swells,
And the beauteous fields of Eden
    Bask beneath the Abbey bells.
Here, where England's statesmen lie,
Listen to a lady's cry.

Gracious Lord, oh bomb the Germans,
    Spare their women for Thy Sake,
And if that is not too easy
    We will pardon Thy Mistake.
But, gracious Lord, whate'er shall be,
Don't let anyone bomb me.


Keep our Empire undismembered
    Guide our Forces by Thy Hand,
Gallant blacks from far Jamaica,
    Honduras and Togoland;
Protect them Lord in all their fights,
And, even more, protect the whites.


Think of what our Nation stands for,
    Books from Boots' and country lanes,
Free speech, free passes, class distinction,
    Democracy and proper drains.
Lord, put beneath Thy special care
One-eighty-nine Cadogan Square.


Although dear Lord I am a sinner,
    I have done no major crime;
Now I'll come to Evening Service
    Whensoever I have the time.
So, Lord, reserve for me a crown,
And do not let my shares go down.


I will labour for Thy Kingdom,
    Help our lads to win the war,
Send white feathers to the cowards,
    Join the Women's Army Corps,
Then wash the Steps around Thy Throne
In the Eternal Safety Zone.


Now I feel a little better,
    What a treat to hear Thy Word,
Where the bones of leading statesmen
    Have so often been interr'd.
And now, dear Lord, I cannot wait
Because I have a luncheon date.

JOHN   BETJEMAN

## Executive

I am a young executive. No cuffs than mine are cleaner;
I have a Slimline brief-case and I use the firm's Cortina.
In every roadside hostelry from here to Burgess Hill
The *maîtres d'hôtel* all know me well and let me sign the bill.

You ask me what it is I do. Well actually, you know,
I'm partly a liaison man and partly P.R.O.
Essentially I integrate the current export drive
And basically I'm viable from ten o'clock till five.

For vital off-the-record work—that's talking transport-wise—
I've a scarlet Aston-Martin—and does she go? She flies!
Pedestrians and dogs and cats—we mark them down for slaughter.
I also own a speed-boat which has never touched the water.

She's built of fibre-glass, of course. I call her 'Mandy Jane'
After a bird I used to know—No soda, please, just plain—
And how did I acquire her? Well to tell you about that
And to put you in the picture I must wear my other hat.

I do some mild developing. The sort of place I need
Is a quiet country market town that's rather run to seed.
A luncheon and a drink or two, a little *savoir faire*—
I fix the Planning Officer, the Town Clerk and the Mayor.

And if some preservationist attempts to interfere
A 'dangerous structure' notice from the Borough Engineer
Will settle any buildings that are standing in our way—
The modern style, sir, with respect, has really come to stay.

JOHN   BETJEMAN

## Money

I sit here eating milk-toast in my lap-robe—
They've got my nightshirt starchier than I told 'em . . . Huh! . . .
I'll tell 'em. . . .
                    Why, I wouldn't have given
A wooden nickel to a wooden Indian, when I began.
I never gave a soul a cent that I could help
That I remember: now I sit here hatching checks
For any mortal cause that writes in asking,
And look or don't look—I've been used to 'em too long—
At seven Corots and the Gobelins
And my first Rembrandt I outbid Clay Frick for:
A dirty Rembrandt bought with dirty money—
But nowadays we've all been to the cleaners'.

(Harriet'd call Miss Tarbell Old Tarbaby—
It none of it will stick, she'd say when I got mad:
And she was right. She always was.)
I used to say I'd made my start in railroads
—'Stocks, that is,' I'd think and never say—
And made my finish in philanthropy:
To think that all along it'uz Service!
I could have kicked myself right in the face
To think I didn't think of that myself. . . .
'There isn't one of you that couldn't have done what I did—'
That was *my* line; and I'd think: 'if you'd been me.'
SEE U.S. LAND OF OPPORTUNITY,
A second-page two-column headline,
Was all I got, most years.

> *They never knew a thing!*

Why, when I think of what I've done, I can't believe it!

. . . A Presbyterian'd say it's Providence.
In my time I've bought the whole Rhode Island Legislature
For—I disremember how much; what for too. . . .
Harriet'd have Nellie Melba in
To entertain our friends—it never entertained *me* none—
And I'd think: 'Birdie, I could buy you
The way you'd buy a piece of Melba toast.'
I had my troubles—nothing money wouldn't cure.
A percentage of the world resented me
There on my money bags in my silk hat.
(To hear Ward I'd still straw stuck in my fur.)
But in the end the money reconciled 'em all.
Don't someone call it the Great Reconciler?
When my boys dynamited thirteen trestles
On the New York Central, I went against my custom then
And told the papers: 'Money's a *responsibility.*'

*I*'d talk down money if I hadn't any. As it was,
The whole office force could hear me through two doors.
E.J. said they said: 'Listen to the Old Man go!'

Why, it was money
That got me shut of my poor trusting wife,
And bought my girl from her, and got me Harriet—
What else would Harriet've married *me* for? . . . She's gone now
And they're gone too, but it's not gone. . . .
You can take it with you anywhere *I*'m going.

. . . While I was looking up my second son-in-law
In Dun and Bradstreet, the social secretary
Came on him in the *Almanach de Gotha.*
It was like I figured, though: he didn't take.

You couldn't tell my grandson from a Frenchman.

And Senators! . . .
     I never saw the man I couldn't buy.

When my Ma died I boarded with a farmer
In the next county; I used to think of her,
And I looked round me, as I could,
And I saw what it added up to: money.
Now I'm dying—I can't call this living—
I haven't any cause to change my mind.
They say that money isn't everything: it isn't;
Money don't help you none when you are sighing
For something else in this wide world to buy. . . .
The first time I couldn't think of anything
I didn't have, it shook me.

      But giving does as well.

       RANDALL   JARRELL


## The Lament of the Banana Man

Gal, I'm tellin' you, I'm tired fo' true,
Tired of Englan', tired o' you.
But I can't go back to Jamaica now . . .

I'm here in Englan', I'm drawin pay,
I go to de underground every day—
Eight hours is all, half-hour fo' lunch,
M' uniform's free, an' m' ticket punch—
Punchin' tickets not hard to do,
When I'm tired o' punchin', I let dem through.

I get a paid holiday once a year.
Ol' age an' sickness can't touch me here.
I have a room of m' own, an' a iron bed,
Dunlopillo under m' head,
A Morphy-Richards to warm de air,
A formica table, an easy chair.
I have summer clothes, an' winter clothes,
An' paper kerchiefs to blow m' nose.

My yoke is easy, my burden is light,
I know a place I can go to, any night,
Dis place Englan'! I'm not complainin',
If it col', it col', if it rainin', it rainin'.

I don't min' if it's mostly night,
Dere's always inside, or de sodium light.
I don't min' white people starin' at me,
Dey don' want me here? Don't is deir country?
You won' catch me bawlin' any homesick tears,
If I don' see Jamaica for a t'ousan' years!

... Gal, I'm tellin' you, I'm tired fo' true,
Tired of Englan', tired o' you,
I can't go back to Jamaica now—
But I'd want to die there, anyhow.

EVAN   JONES

## Meeting of Strangers

'Nice jacket you gat deh, man!'

He swerved his bicycle toward my curb
to call   then flashed round the corner
a blur in the dusk   of somebody big
redshirted   young   dark   unsmiling

As I stood waiting for a taxi to show
I thought him droll at least
A passing pleasantry?   It was frayed
a sixdollar coat   tropical weight
in this heat only something with pockets
to carry things in

Now all four streets were empty
Dockland   everything shut

It was a sound no bigger than a breath
that made me wheel

He was ten feet away   redshirt
The cycle leant by a post farther off
where an alley came in   What?!

My turning froze him
in the middle of some elaborate stealth
He looked almost comic   splayed
but there was a glitter
under the downheld hand
and something smoked from his eyes

By God if I was going to be stabbed
for my wallet (adrenalin suffused me)
it would have to be done in plain sight
I made a flying leap
to the middle of the crossing
White man   tourist   surrogate   yes
but not guilty enough
to be skewered in the guts for it
without raising all Trinidad first
with shouts   fists   feet   whatever
—I squared round to meet him

and there was a beautiful taxi
lumbering in from a sidestreet
empty!

As I rolled away    safe as Elijah
lucky as Ganymede
there on the curb I'd leaped from
stood that damned cyclist solemnly
shouting

'What did he say?' I asked the driver
He shrugged at the windshield
'Man dat a crazy boogoo
He soun like he say
"dat a nice jump you got too" '

                              EARLE  BIRNEY


## Barn Owl

Daybreak: the household slept.
I rose before the sun.
A horny fiend, I crept
out with my father's gun.
Let him dream of a child
obedient, angel-mild—

no No-sayer, robbed of power
by sleep. I knew my prize
who swooped home at this hour
with daylight-riddled eyes
to his place on a high beam
in our old stables, to dream

light's useless time away.
I stood, holding my breath,
in urine-scented hay,
master of life and death,
a wisp-haired judge whose law
would punish beak and claw.

My first shot struck. He swayed,
ruined, beating his only
wing as I watched, afraid
by the fallen gun, a lonely
child who believed death clean
and final, not the obscene

bundle of stuff that dropped,
and dribbled through loose straw
tangling its bowels, and hopped
blindly closer. I saw
those eyes that did not see
mirror my cruelty

while the wrecked thing that could
not bear the light nor hide
hobbled in its own blood.
My father reached my side,
gave me the fallen gun.
'End what you have begun.'

I fired. The blank eyes shone
once into mine, and slept.
I leaned my head upon
my father's arm, and wept
owl-blind in morning sun
for what I had begun.

GWEN HARWOOD

## Cross-Reference

I am a good Australian. I intend
to educate my kids with Time-Life Books.
They'll understand the Arizona desert,
know the buttes and mesas, walk
the rims of canyons in their play.
Near Moab, Utah, is a natural arch,

the longest yet discovered. Joshua trees
need cold, will only grow in deserts
at elevations of two thousand feet.
This will be the lore we know,
the Nature Library Book of Deserts
through and threadbare through.

When we're out past Rockleigh sometimes
we walk hills and creeks, observe
eroded gullies laid like textbooks
on the slopes. They're only six feet deep,
quite young (an unwise plough, or sheep track,
started them) and we peruse and learn
the shapes of water worn on banks, cut clay,
the pink quartz caps of pillar, ridge,
and stack. Our frames of reference are right:
Time-Life, Dakota, all the Kodak skill
of boxed and polished Badlands, on this hill.

JOHN   GRIFFIN

## The Trees: A Convict Monologue

1.
I move sharp, not too fancy or nice—a lurch,
a curse, a getaway. They called me mudsplash
but I was quicker: my eyes have been everywhere
two jumps before you.
What a laugh to be flicked in for passing forged currency!
I'm still laughing—rather laugh than dance, I tell you.
The others were fools on the convictship, but I rubbed close in
just for the mansmell, to remind myself we were still living.
My guts ache most for the people-breath of streets:
while I was free I never left the city but once—
shit, the stink of countryside! air to blast your snotholes
fill you full of bush and breeze and bloody distances.
The only good thing was it taught me, then,
that even air is special: one gulp and you know
you are home in my lovely broken-mouthed slut city.

2.
I got used to chains. There were always others
near enough to hit and to hurt and to squeeze in to;
I tell you I was sharper than the rest, I was patient.
And I was high on the good list, none of your grumble
and blood. I joked like the city,
I made them laugh and remember—but no commerce named;
in two years I negotiated my sentence for a good kitchen,
with a wench there one of the prettier bitches.
I used her. And the master was, well, I had hopes.

3.
But, after the barracks and sturdy crush of quarters, the open
unnerved me, I had not planned on that—the just nothing
of hills, hollows, ridges. Nobody told me trees watched,
connived, were not still, were never still.
They rubbed, they grew blisters like their blistered leaves.
At first, night-time, listen, something about aloneness,
but later, even at day, it was voices no one could live with,
not human: earth, decay, silences. That was it—silence
speaking to me. I did not scream. Rubbing. Suddenly
to wake trapped, held down in nothing but emptiness
and to run screaming, voice rattling to drown that foreignness
till the cavities of the head were cities of yell myself myself
all through the too bright moonsilence and the hallways.
And then ropes and then whips beat me sensible.
I am recovered. I will cut down every tree,
every one. I will be invincible.

THOMAS   SHAPCOTT

## The Lotos-Eaters

'Courage!' he said, and pointed toward the land,
'This mounting wave will roll us shoreward soon.'
In the afternoon they came unto a land
In which it seemed always afternoon.
All round the coast the languid air did swoon,
Breathing like one that hath a weary dream.
Full-faced above the valley stood the moon;
And like a downward smoke, the slender stream
Along the cliff to fall and pause and fall did seem.

A land of streams! some, like a downward smoke,
Slow-dropping veils of thinnest lawn, did go;
And some thro' wavering lights and shadows broke,
Rolling a slumbrous sheet of foam below.
They saw the gleaming river seaward flow
From the inner land: far off, three mountain-tops,
Three silent pinnacles of aged snow,
Stood sunset-flushed: and, dewed with showery drops,
Up-clomb the shadowy pine above the woven copse.

The charmed sunset lingered low adown
In the red West: thro' mountain clefts the dale
Was seen far inland, and the yellow down
Bordered with palm, and many a winding vale
And meadow, set with slender galingale;
A land where all things always seemed the same!
And round about the keel with faces pale,
Dark faces pale against that rosy flame,
The mild-eyed melancholy Lotos-eaters came.

Branches they bore of that enchanted stem,
Laden with flower and fruit, whereof they gave
To each, but whoso did receive of them,
And taste, to him the gushing of the wave
Far far away did seem to mourn and rave
On alien shores; and if his fellow spake,
His voice was thin, as voices from the grave;
And deep-asleep he seemed, yet all awake,
And music in his ears his beating heart did make.

They sat them down upon the yellow sand,
Between the sun and moon upon the shore;
And sweet it was to dream of Fatherland,
Of child, and wife, and slave; but evermore
Most weary seemed the sea, weary the oar,
Weary the wandering fields of barren foam.
Then some one said, 'We will return no more;'
And all at once they sang, 'Our island home
Is far beyond the wave; we will no longer roam.'

**Choric Song**

I

There is sweet music here that softer falls
Than petals from blown roses on the grass,
Or night-dews on still waters between walls
Of shadowy granite, in a gleaming pass;
Music that gentlier on the spirit lies,
Than tired eyelids upon tired eyes;
Music that brings sweet sleep down from the blissful skies.
Here are cool mosses deep,
And thro' the moss the ivies creep,
And in the stream the long-leaved flowers weep,
And from the craggy ledge the poppy hangs in sleep.

II

Why are we weighed upon with heaviness,
And utterly consumed with sharp distress,
While all things else have rest from weariness?

All things have rest: why should we toil alone,
We only toil, who are the first of things,
And make perpetual moan,
Still from one sorrow to another thrown:
Nor ever fold our wings,
And cease from wanderings,
Nor steep our brows in slumber's holy balm;
Nor harken what the inner spirit sings,
'There is no joy but calm!'
Why should we only toil, the roof and crown of things?

III

Lo! in the middle of the wood,
The folded leaf is wooed from out the bud
With winds upon the branch, and there
Grows green and broad, and takes no care,
Sun-steeped at noon, and in the moon
Nightly dew-fed; and turning yellow
Falls, and floats adown the air.
Lo! sweetened with the summer light,
The full-juiced apple, waxing over-mellow,
Drops in a silent autumn night.
All its allotted length of days,
The flower ripens in its place,
Ripens and fades, and falls, and hath no toil,
Fast-rooted in the fruitful soil.

IV

Hateful is the dark-blue sky,
Vaulted o'er the dark-blue sea.
Death is the end of life; ah, why
Should life all labour be?
Let us alone. Time driveth onward fast,
And in a little while our lips are dumb.
Let us alone. What is it that will last?
All things are taken from us, and become
Portions and parcels of the dreadful Past.
Let us alone. What pleasure can we have
To war with evil? is there any peace
In ever climbing up the climbing wave?
All things have rest, and ripen toward the grave
In silence; ripen, fall and cease:
Give us long rest or death, dark death, or dreamful ease.

V

How sweet it were, hearing the downward stream,
With half-shut eyes ever to seem
Falling asleep in a half-dream!
To dream and dream, like yonder amber light,
Which will not leave the myrrh-bush on the height;
To hear each other's whispered speech;

Eating the Lotos day by day,
To watch the crisping ripples on the beach,
And tender curving lines of creamy spray;
To lend our hearts and spirits wholly
To the influence of mild-minded melancholy;
To muse and brood and live again in memory,
With those old faces of our infancy
Heaped over with a mound of grass,
Two handfuls of white dust, shut in an urn of brass!

VI

Dear is the memory of our wedded lives,
And dear the last embraces of our wives
And their warm tears: but all hath suffered change:
For surely now our household hearths are cold:
Our sons inherit us: our looks are strange:
And we should come like ghosts to trouble joy.
Or else the island princes over-bold
Have eat our substance, and the minstrel sings
Before them of the ten years' war in Troy,
And our great deeds, as half-forgotten things.
Is there confusion in the little isle?
Let what is broken so remain.
The Gods are hard to reconcile:
'Tis hard to settle order once again.
There *is* confusion worse than death,
Trouble on trouble, pain on pain,
Long labour unto aged breath,
Sore task to hearts worn out by many wars
And eyes grown dim with gazing on the pilot-stars.

VII

But, propt on beds of amaranth and moly,
How sweet (while warm airs lull us, blowing lowly)
With half-dropt eyelid still,
Beneath a heaven dark and holy,
To watch the long bright river drawing slowly
His waters from the purple hill—
To hear the dewy echoes calling
From cave to cave thro' the thick-twined vine—
To watch the emerald-coloured water falling
Thro' many a woven acanthus-wreath divine!
Only to hear and see the far-off sparkling brine,
Only to hear were sweet, stretched out beneath the pine.

VIII

The Lotos blooms below the barren peak:
The Lotos blows by every winding creek:
All day the wind breathes low with mellower tone:
Thro' every hollow cave and alley lone

Round and round the spicy downs the yellow Lotos-dust is blown.
We have had enough of action, and of motion we,
Rolled to starboard, rolled to larboard, when the surge was seething free,
Where the wallowing monster spouted his foam-fountains in the sea.
Let us swear an oath, and keep it with an equal mind,
In the hollow Lotos-land to live and lie reclined
On the hills like Gods together, careless of mankind.
For they lie beside their nectar, and the bolts are hurled
Far below them in the valleys, and the clouds are lightly curled
Round their golden houses, girdled with the gleaming world:
Where they smile in secret, looking over wasted lands,
Blight and famine, plague and earthquake, roaring deeps and fiery sands,
Clanging fights, and flaming towns, and sinking ships, and praying hands.
But they smile, they find a music centred in a doleful song
Steaming up, a lamentation and an ancient tale of wrong,
Like a tale of little meaning tho' the words are strong;
Chanted from an ill-used race of men that cleave the soil,
Sow the seed, and reap the harvest with enduring toil,
Storing yearly little dues of wheat, and wine and oil;
Till they perish and they suffer—some, 'tis whispered— down in hell
Suffer endless anguish, others in Elysian valleys dwell,
Resting weary limbs at last on beds of asphodel.
Surely, surely, slumber is more sweet than toil, the shore
Than labour in the deep mid-ocean, wind and wave and oar;
Oh rest ye, brother mariners, we will not wander more.

ALFRED, LORD TENNYSON

# Reflective Verse

In a famous passage, Wordsworth said that poetry takes its origin from emotion recollected in tranquillity. This may not be true of all poetry, but in many poems we are aware that the poet is reflecting and meditating on the significance of an experience, either present or past. In some cases the reflections are very personal, in others they are more general and in yet others they are distinctly religious or philosophic.

Wordsworth's reflective lyric 'Lines Written in Early Spring' shows how easily and naturally a purely personal experience on a particular day can lead to general reflections on man and nature. If we were not led through a train of thoughts and emotions by the imagery and if we were not made to feel that the poet was struggling with irrational conclusions ('And I must think, do all I can'), the ending might seem too forced and moralistic.

> If this belief from heaven be sent,
> If such be Nature's holy plan,
> Have I not reason to lament
> What man has made of man.

The movement from the particular to the general takes a different course in Yeats's 'The Wild Swans at Coole'. The poet's meditation begins by being quite personal and specific, related to seeing swans on two occasions separated by nineteen years. The reflections gradually become more general as the swans acquire symbolic status. Finally they come to represent a permanent order of beauty, love and procreation in contrast to the aging man's sense of impermanence and change. The contrasted images and rhythms of the poem reconcile opposites: urgent movement with calm repose, the sense of loss with gained maturity of vision. Through reflection then comes wisdom.

In a number of poems in this section the poet reflects on the art he practises;

he considers what it is to be a poet. A very modern instance is Michael Dransfield's 'Like This for Years', a bitter and sardonic reflection on how a young Australian poet feels 'alone in a desert full of strangers'. By contrast James McAuley's lyric 'To any Poet' celebrates the joy of poetic creation without any qualifying sense that the Australian environment is unfavourable to the poet.

Poets are affected by the age in which they live. George Herbert's seventeenth-century metaphysical lyric is typical of an age of religious faith in its serene untroubled beauty:

Only a sweet and virtuous soul,
Like seasoned timber never gives;
But though the whole world turn to coal,
   Then chiefly lives.

By contrast, Matthew Arnold's Dover Beach' typifies an age of religious doubt, when 'the Sea of Faith' is retreating 'down the vast edges drear/And naked shingles of the world', while Edward Thomas in 'Lights Out' and Yeats in 'Death' express a characteristically modern stoicism in the face of death and the unknown. Even more modern in its witty irreverence is D.J. Enright's 'Small Oratorio'.

Let there be pie
In the sky
When I die

Many of the reflections in the poems in this section are unpredictable and lighthearted. For Judith Rodriguez, a centipede sets off the most unexpected train of thought, while B.L. Taylor's amusing meditations on the star Canopus help to put the whole world of politics into proper perspective. Two poems, Ian Reid's 'Beached' and Geoffrey Dutton's 'The Island Day', provide an illuminating comparison. In the first, the New Zealand poet's ordinary experience of wading in the sea on an Australian beach unexpectedly prompts deep reflections on what it is to belong anywhere. In the second, reflections on a day at the beach range more widely but more predictably to encompass all those things that have become associated with the two lovers' day of joy.

Two poems, one by the modern Australian poet Les A. Murray and the other by the English Romantic poet Coleridge, illustrate how often the reflective poem assumes a circular pattern, beginning with a scene or object observed by the poet and finally returning to it. In Murray's 'Noonday Axeman', which presents the meditations of a thoughtful countryman, the last line 'I shoulder my axe and set off home through the stillness' re-echoes the noonday stillness of the opening scene. Similarly, in Coleridge's 'Frost at Midnight', after the long middle section reflecting on the poet's boyhood and his hopes for his son cradled by his side, the poem returns us to the opening silent frosty scene. But by the time the poem comes full circle we realise that the poet has completed a voyage of self-discovery. He returns to the original scene with added insight and wisdom.

Tones vary from poem to poem and within individual poems, but the prevailing tone is that of thoughtful introspection. There is often a characteristic movement inwards from the object or experience that first prompted the poet's meditation to the deepest recesses of the poet's mind. All these poems in their different ways tell us something about the balance that has to be achieved, for the poet and all of us, between the outer world and the inner world, between the seen and the unseen, between the temporary and the eternal.

### Noonday Axeman

Axe-fall, echo and silence. Noonday silence.
Two miles from here, it is the twentieth century:
cars on the bitumen, powerline vaulting the farms.
Here, with my axe, I am chopping into the stillness.

Axe-fall, echo and silence. I pause, roll tobacco,
twist a cigarette, lick it. All is still.
I lean on my axe. A cloud of fragrant leaves
hangs over me moveless, pierced everywhere by sky.

Here, I remember all of a hundred years:
candleflame, still night, frost and cattle bells,
the draywheels' silence final in our ears,
and the first red cattle spreading through the hills

and my great-great-grandfather here with his first sons,
who would grow old, still speaking with his Scots accent,
having never seen those highlands that they sang of . . .
a hundred years. I stand and smoke in the silence.

A hundred years of clearing, splitting, sawing,
a hundred years of timbermen, ringbarkers, fencers
and women in kitchens, stoking loud iron stoves
year in, year out, and singing old songs to their children

have made this silence human and familiar
no farther than where the farms rise into foothills,
and, in that time, how many have sought their graves
or fled to the cities, maddened by this stillness?

Between the trees, the tall light reaches me.
Things are what they are, and that is frightening:
they require obedience, if they are to be mastered
and so many have tried to force their dreams on this plant.

Things are so wordless. These two opposing scarves
I have cut in my red-gum squeeze out jewels of sap
and stare. And soon, with a few more axe-strokes,
the tree will grow troubled, tremble, shift its crown

and, leaning slowly, gather speed and colossally
crash down and lie between the standing trunks.
And then, I know, of the knowledge that led my forebears
to drink and black rage and wordlessness, there will be silence.

After the tree falls, there will reign the same silence
as stuns and spurs us, enraptures and defeats us,
as seems to some a challenge, and seems to others
to be waiting here for something beyond imagining.

Axe-fall, echo and silence. Unhuman silence.
A stone cracks in the heat. Through the still twigs, radiance
stings at my eyes. I rub a damp brow with a handkerchief
and chop on into the stillness. Axe-fall and echo.

The great mast murmurs now. The scarves in its trunk
crackle and squeak now, crack and increase as the hushing
weight of high branches heels outward, and commences
tearing and falling, and the collapse is tremendous.

Twigs fly, leaves puff and subside. The severed trunk
slips off its stump and drops upon its shadow . . .
And then there is no more. The stillness is there
as ever. And I fall to lopping branches.

Axe-fall, echo and silence. It will be centuries
before many men are truly at home in this country,
and yet, there have always been some, in each generation,
there have always been some who could live in the presence of silence.

And some, I have known them, men with gentle broad hands,
who would die if removed from these unpeopled places,
some again I have seen, bemused and shy in the cities,
you have built against silence, dumbly trudging through noise

past the railway stations, looking up through the traffic
at the smoky halls, dreaming of journeys, of stepping
down fron the train at some upland stop to recover
the crush of dry grass underfoot, the silence of trees.

Axe-fall, echo and silence. Dreaming silence.
Though I myself run to the cities, I will forever
be coming back here to walk, knee-deep in ferns,
up and away from his metropolitan century,

to remember my ancestors, axemen, dairymen, horse-breakers,
now coffined in silence, down with their beards and dreams,
who, unwilling or rapt, despairing or very patient,
made what amounts to a human breach in the silence,

made of their lives the rough foundation of legends—
men must have legends, else they will die of strangeness—
then died in their turn, each, after his own fashion,
resigned or agonized, from silence into great silence.

Axe-fall, echo and axe-fall. Noonday silence.
Though I go to the cities, turning my back on these hills,
for the talk and dazzle of cities, for the sake of belonging
for months and years at a time to the twentieth century,

the city will never quite hold me. I will be always
coming back here on the up-train, peering, leaning
out of the window to see, on far-off ridges
the sky between the trees, and over the racket
of the rails to hear the echo and the silence.

I shoulder my axe and set off home through the stillness.

LES A. MURRAY

## Frost at Midnight

The Frost performs its secret ministry,
Unhelped by any wind. The owlet's cry
Came loud—and hark, again! loud as before.
The inmates of my cottage, all at rest,
Have left me to that solitude, which suits
Abstruser musings: save that at my side
My cradled infant slumbers peacefully.
'Tis calm indeed! so calm, that it disturbs
And vexes meditation with its stange
And extreme silentness. Sea, hill, and wood,
This populous village! Sea, and hill, and wood,
With all the numberless goings-on of life,
Inaudible as dreams! the thin blue flame
Lies on my low-burnt fire, and quivers not;
Only that film, which fluttered on the grate,
Still flutters there, the sole unquiet thing.

Methinks, its motion in this hush of nature
Gives it dim sympathies with me who live,
Making it a companionable form,
Whose puny flaps and freaks the idling Spirit
By its own moods interprets, everywhere
Echo or mirror seeking of itself,
And makes a toy of Thought.
                              But O! how oft,
How oft, at school, with most believing mind,
Presageful, have I gazed upon the bars,
To watch that fluttering *stranger!* and as oft
With unclosed lids, already had I dreamt
Of my sweet birth-place, and the old church-tower,
Whose bells, the poor man's only music, rang
From morn to evening, all the hot Fair-day,
So sweetly, that they stirred and haunted me
With a wild pleasure, falling on mine ear
Most like articulate sounds of things to come!
So gazed I, till the soothing things, I dreamt,
Lulled me to sleep, and sleep prolonged my dreams!
And so I brooded all the following morn,
Awed by the stern preceptor's face, mine eye
Fixed with mock study on my swimming book:
Save if the door half opened, and I snatched
A hasty glance, and still my heart leaped up,
For still I hoped to see the *stranger's* face,
Townsman, or aunt, or sister more beloved,
My play-mate when we both were clothed alike!


    Dear Babe, that sleepest cradled by my side,
Whose gentle breathings, heard in this deep calm,
Fill up the interspersèd vacancies
And momentary pauses of the thought!
My babe so beautiful! it thrills my heart
With tender gladness, thus to look at thee,
And think that thou shalt learn far other lore,
And in far other scenes! For I was reared
In the great city, pent 'mid cloisters dim,
And saw nought lovely but the sky and stars.
But *thou,* my babe! shalt wander like a breeze
By lakes and sandy shores, beneath the crags
Of ancient mountain, and beneath the clouds,
Which image in their bulk both lakes and shores
And mountain crags: so shalt thou see and hear
The lovely shapes and sounds intelligible
Of that eternal language, which thy God
Utters, who from eternity doth teach
Himself in all, and all things in himself.
Great universal Teacher! he shall mould
Thy spirit, and by giving make it ask.

Therefore all seasons shall be sweet to thee,
Whether the summer clothe the general earth
With greenness, or the redbreast sit and sing
Betwixt the tufts of snow on the bare branch
Of mossy apple-tree, while the nigh thatch
Smokes in the sun-thaw; whether the eave-drops fall
Heard only in the trances of the blast,
Or if the secret ministry of frost
Shall hang them up in silent icicles,
Quietly shining to the quiet Moon.

SAMUEL TAYLOR COLERIDGE

## The Island Day

No day ever began like this.
The sun our love, the sea our kiss,
The shells of night upon the beach
Are mysteries within our reach.
A blue wren on a broken tree,
Brighter than this clear sky could be,
Sings that silence must be broken,
That we must keep this day as token
Of all the days since we were lovers.

This island that our love discovers,
Blessed by sun and windless air,
Shall for one perfect day we share
Be lapped by seas of happiness,
Guarded by sands of idleness.
The hungry ocean shall be fed,
The gales, like us, lie soft in bed.
Fan-shells and cowries on the sand
Shall wait below your gentle hand,
The bottlebrush in flower shall burn
On every tree when you return.

If I were time's geographer
This island day I would confer
On you, and your gift would be mine.
Why can we not make one day fine?
Oh, we have no control at all
Of things that we find magical.
The morning's calm is blown by noon,
Clouds wrap the sun, the bird-song soon
Grates to the cruelty of the crow,
The flowers are stripped till the twigs show,
And the sea throws high upon the sand
Drops salt as tears that flow on land.

GEOFFREY DUTTON

### Dover Beach

The sea is calm to-night.
The tide is full, the moon lies fair
Upon the straits;—on the French coast the light
Gleams and is gone; the cliffs of England stand,
Glimmering and vast, out in the tranquil bay.
Come to the window, sweet is the night air!
Only, from the long line of spray
Where the sea meets the moon-blanched land,
Listen! you hear the grating roar
Of pebbles which the waves draw back, and fling,
At their return, up the high strand,
Begin, and cease, and then again begin,
With tremulous cadence slow, and bring
The eternal note of sadness in.

Sophocles long ago
Heard it on the Aegean, and it brought
Into his mind the turbid ebb and flow
Of human misery; we
Find also in the sound a thought,
Hearing it by this distant northern sea.

The Sea of Faith
Was once, too, at the full, and round earth's shore
Lay like the folds of a bright girdle furled.
But now I only hear
Its melancholy, long, withdrawing roar,
Retreating, to the breath
Of the night-wind, down the vast edges drear
And naked shingles of the world.

Ah, love, let us be true
To one another! for the world, which seems
To lie before us like a land of dreams,
So various, so beautiful, so new,
Hath really neither joy, nor love, nor light,
Nor certitude, nor peace, nor help for pain;
And we are here as on a darkling plain
Swept with confused alarms of struggle and flight,
Where ignorant armies clash by night.

MATTHEW   ARNOLD

### Beached

Friday, on the beach—and the footprint
is mine, filling slowly with foamy water
that may have slipped past Island Bay
              slopped around Banks Peninsula
on its way here to seep into these toe-marks.

To have made the Tasman crossing
is one thing; it's another
to step firmly ashore.
Scuffing through shifty water-margins you've got to admit
that years after landfall there's no assurance
of having both feet on this or any ground.
Right now, just five toes are impressive.

I paddle over pebbles,
bones of contentment
sucked at by sea-lip:
their glow is outlandish

till waves withdraw, leave them
to sun and sand. Lustre
drains away; they are dingy stones.

Belonging is an elementary matter.
Longing is its echo, on the ebb.

IAN   REID

## Autobiography

Time holds the glass the wrong way round:
I see a matchstick child, thin,
Dwindling through far-off summer days
Exhausted in a cotton dress,
Sustained by longing, burning still
With passion underneath the skin
For love, for words, for excellence.

She crouches over poetry,
Starts like a bird and trembling waits
The lightning-flash of love, exchange
Of name for name and known for known.
She learns that word and love are one
Though each assume a different form,
And she the seeker and the sought.

The good, indifferent and bad
She takes with equal joy, content
That all are shaped like poetry
And all can teach her excellence.
Now, chin on hand, I watch her make
Her wilful way to where I am.
How thin she is ! How thin and grave!

ROSEMARY   DOBSON

## The Wild Swans at Coole

The trees are in their autumn beauty,
The woodland paths are dry,
Under the October twilight the water
Mirrors a still sky;
Upon the brimming water among the stones
Are nine-and-fifty swans.

The nineteenth autumn has come upon me
Since I first made my count;
I saw, before I had well finished,
All suddenly mount
And scatter wheeling in great broken rings
Upon their clamorous wings.

I have looked upon those brilliant creatures,
And now my heart is sore.
All's changed since I, hearing at twilight,
The first time on this shore,
The bell-beat of their wings above my head,
Trod with a lighter tread.

Unwearied still, lover by lover,
They paddle in the cold
Companionable streams or climb the air;
Their hearts have got grown old;
Passion or conquest, wander where they will,
Attend upon them still.

But now they drift on the still water,
Mysterious, beautiful;
Among what rushes will they build,
By what lake's edge or pool
Delight men's eyes when I awake some day
To find they have flown away?

W.B. YEATS

## Helen

And you, Helen, what should I give you?
So many things I would give you
Had I an infinite great store
Offered me and I stood before
To choose. I would give you youth,
All kinds of loveliness and truth,
A clear eye as good as mine,
Lands, waters, flowers, wine,
As many children as your heart
Might wish for, a far better art

Than mine can be, all you have lost
Upon the travelling waters tossed,
Or given to me. If I could choose
Freely in that great treasure-house
Anything from any shelf,
I would give you back yourself,
And power to discriminate
What you want and want it not too late,
Many fair days free from care
And heart to enjoy both foul and fair,
And myself, too, if I could find
Where it lay hidden and it proved kind.

EDWARD THOMAS

## A Valediction: Forbidding Mourning

As virtuous men pass mildly away,
  And whisper to their souls to go,
Whilst some of their sad friends do say,
  'The breath goes now,' and some say, 'No:'

So let us melt, and make no noise,
  No tear-floods, nor sigh-tempests move;
'Twere profanation of our joys
  To tell the laity our love.

Moving of th' earth brings harms and fears;
  Men reckon what it did, and meant;
But trepidation of the spheres,
  Though greater far, is innocent.

Dull sublunary lovers' love
  (Whose soul is sense) cannot admit
Absence, because it doth remove
  Those things which elemented it.

But we by a love, so much refin'd,
  That ourselves know not what it is,
Inter-assured of the mind,
  Care less eyes, lips, and hands to miss.

Our two souls therefore, which are one,
  Though I must go, endure not yet
A breach, but an expansion,
  Like gold to aery thinness beat.

If they be two, they are two so
  As stiff twin compasses are two,
Thy soul the fix'd foot, makes no show
  To move, but doth, if th' other do.

And though it in the centre sit,
  Yet when the other far doth roam,
It leans, and hearkens after it,
  And grows erect, as that comes home.

Such wilt thou be to me, who must
  Like th' other foot, obliquely run;
Thy firmness draws my circle just,
  And makes me end, where I begun.

JOHN   DONNE

## Meditation on a Bone

*A piece of bone, found at Trondhjem in 1902,*
*with the following runic inscription*
*(about A.D. 1050) cut on it:*
*'I loved her as a maiden;*
*I will not trouble Erlend's detestable wife;*
*better she should be a widow.'*

Words scored upon a bone,
Scratched in despair or rage—
Nine hundred years have gone;
Now, in another age,
They burn with passion on
A scholar's tranquil page.

The scholar takes his pen
And turns the bone about,
And writes those words again.
Once more they seethe and shout,
And through a human brain
Undying hate rings out.

'I loved her when a maid;
I loathe and love the wife
That warms another's bed:
*Let him beware his life!'*
The scholar's hand is stayed;
His pen becomes a knife

To grave in living bone
The fierce archaic cry.
He sits and reads his own
Dull sum of misery.
A thousand years have flown
Before that ink is dry.

And, in a foreign tongue,
A man, who is not he,
Reads and his heart is wrung
This ancient grief to see,
And thinks: When I am dung,
What bone shall speak for me?

A.D. HOPE

## Like This for Years

In the cold weather
the cold city the cold
heart of something as pitiless as apathy
to be a poet in Australia
is the ultimate commitment.

When y've been thrown out of the last car
for speaking truthfully or mumbling poems
and the emptiness is not these stranded
endless plains but knowing that you are completely
alone in a desert full of strangers

and when the waves cast you up who sought
to dive so deep and come up with
more than water in yr hands
and the water itself is sand is air is something
unholdable

you realise that what you taste now in the mornings
is not so much blood as the failure of language
and no good comes of singing or of silence
the trees wont hold you you reject rejection
and the ultimate commitment
is survival

MICHAEL   DRANSFIELD

## Pas de Deux for Lovers

Morning ought not
to be complex.
The sun is a seed
cast at dawn into the long
furrow of history.

To wake
and go
would be so simple.

Yet

how the
first light
makes gold her hair

upon my arm.
How then
shall I leave.
and where away to go. Day
is so deep already with involvement.

MICHAEL DRANSFIELD

## Centipede

Sat in my red room with a centipede,
I've no idea when he'll come out:
from the spine of which book,
from the entrails of which chair.
But he's there.

I flapped the slats of a plastic fly-swat
at his multitudinous crescent on the floor.
I had never seen a centipede before.
His fringe of oars surged on in clumps, he veered
and vanished.

Since then I have worn shoes to sit at my desk.
My study attends him, supine and suburban
to his glamour of fangs, his avenue of legs,
the spans of his back and his multiple head in procession.
What has happened

is that till the world's ribs unfasten we closet together,
he and I, eye to eye, prospecting our plaster crevice.
Though I looked up his Latin and habits, not niched in a book
nor tacking a threadbare lap of blue-matted floor
he shines now,

but steers all levels to the abominable fall
that is fear. A finger's-length of segments rustling
with centipede intent, stirs in my head;
dark jewel, he has always festered there.
I scan my wall.

JUDITH   RODRIGUEZ

## Lines Written in Early Spring

I heard a thousand blended notes,
While in a grove I sate reclined,
In that sweet mood when pleasant thoughts
Bring sad thoughts to the mind.

To her fair works did Nature link
The human soul that through me ran;
And much it grieved my heart to think
What man has made of man.

Through primrose tufts, in that green bower,
The periwinkle trailed its wreaths;
And 'tis my faith that every flower
Enjoys the air it breathes.

The birds around me hopped and played,
Their thoughts I cannot measure: —
But the least motion which they made,
It seemed a thrill of pleasure.

The budding twigs spread out their fan,
To catch the breezy air;
And I must think, do all I can,
That there was pleasure there.

If this belief from heaven be sent,
If such be Nature's holy plan,
Have I not reason to lament
What man has made of man?

WILLIAM   WORDSWORTH

## To Any Poet

Take salt upon your tongue.
And do not feed the heart
With sorrow, darkness or lies:
These are the death of art.

Living is thirst for joy;
That is what art rehearses.
Let sober drunkenness give
Its splendour to your verses.

Move like the sable swan
On the luminous expanse:
In sight but out of range
Of barking ignorance.

JAMES McAULEY

## *from* Rubaiyát of Omár Khayyám of Naishápúr

1

Awake! for Morning in the Bowl of Night
Has flung the Stone that puts the Stars to Flight:
And Lo! the Hunter of the East has caught
The Sultan's Turret in a Noose of Light.

2

Dreaming when Dawn's Left Hand was in the Sky
I heard a Voice within the Tavern cry,
'Awake, my Little ones, and fill the Cup
Before Life's Liquor in its Cup be dry!'

3

And, as the Cock crew, those who stood before
The Tavern shouted—'Open then the Door!
You know how little while we have to stay,
And, once departed, may return no more.'

*

9

But come with old Khayyám, and leave the Lot
Of Kaikobád and Kaikhosrú forgot:
Let Rustum lay about him as he will,
Or Hátim Tai cry Supper—heed them not.

10

With me along some Strip of Herbage strown
That just divides the desert from the sown,
Where name of Slave and Sultan scarce is known,
And pity Sultan Máhmúd on his Throne.


11

Here with a Loaf of Bread beneath the Bough,
A Flask of Wine, a Book of Verse—and Thou
Beside me singing in the Wilderness—
And Wilderness is Paradise enow.


12

'How sweet is mortal Sovranty'—think some:
Others—'How blest the Paradise to come!'
Ah, take the Cash in hand and waive the Rest;
Oh, the brave Music of a *distant* Drum!


\*


16

Think, in this batter'd Caravanserai
Whose Doorways are alternate Night and Day,
How Sultan after Sultan with his Pomp
Abode his Hour or two, and went his way.


17

They say the Lion and the Lizard keep
The Courts where Jamshýd gloried and drank deep;
And Bahrám, that great Hunter—the Wild Ass
Stamps o'er his Head, and he lies fast asleep.


18

I sometimes think that never blows so red
The Rose as where some buried Caesar bled;
That every Hyacinth the Garden wears
Dropt in its Lap from some once lovely Head.


19

And this delightful Herb whose tender Green
Fledges the River's Lip on which we lean—
Ah, lean upon it lightly! for who knows
From what once lovely Lip it springs unseen!


20

Ah, my Belovéd, fill the Cup that clears
To-day of past Regrets and future Fears—
*To-morrow?*—Why, To-morrow I may be
Myself with Yesterday's Seven Thousand Years.


\*

24

Alike for those who for To-day prepare,
And those that after a To-morrow stare,
A Muezzín from the Tower of Darkness cries
'Fools! your Reward is neither Here nor There!'

25

Why, all the Saints and Sages who discussed
Of the Two Worlds so learnedly, are thrust
Like foolish Prophets forth; their Words to Scorn
Are scattered, and their Mouths are stopped with Dust.

26

Oh, come with old Khayyám, and leave the Wise
To talk; one thing is certain, that Life flies;
One thing is certain, and the Rest is Lies;
The Flower that once has blown for ever dies.

27

Myself when young did eagerly frequent
Doctor and Saint, and heard great Argument
About it and about: but evermore
Came out by the same Door as in I went.

28

With them the Seed of Wisdom did I sow,
And with my own hand laboured it to grow:
And this was all the Harvest that I reaped—
'I came like Water, and like Wind I go.'

29

Into this Universe, and *why* not knowing,
Nor *whence,* like Water willy-nilly flowing:
And out of it, as Wind along the Waste,
I know not *whither,* willy-nilly blowing.

*

51

The Moving Finger writes; and having writ,
Moves on: nor all thy Piety nor Wit
Shall lure it back to cancel half a Line,
Nor all thy Tears wash out a Word of it.

*

72

Alas, that Spring should vanish with the Rose!
That Youth's sweet-scented Manuscript should close!
The Nightingale that in the Branches sang,
Ah, whence, and whither flown again, who knows!

73

Ah Love! could thou and I with Fate conspire
To grasp this sorry Scheme of Things entire,
Would we not shatter it to bits—and then
Re-mould it nearer to the Heart's Desire!

74

Ah, Moon of my Delight who know'st no wane,
The Moon of Heaven is rising once again:
How oft hereafter rising shall she look
Through this same Garden after me—in vain!

75

And when Thyself with shining Foot shall pass
Among the Guests star-scattered on the Grass,
And in thy joyous Errand reach the Spot
Where I made one—turn down an empty Glass!

EDWARD   FITZGERALD

## A Summer Night

In the deserted, moon-blanched street,
How lonely rings the echo of my feet!
Those windows, which I gaze at, frown,
Silent and white, unopening down,
Repellent as the world; but see,
A break between the housetops shows
The moon! and lost behind her, fading dim
Into the dewy dark obscurity
Down at the far horizon's rim,
Doth a whole tract of heaven disclose!

And to my mind the thought
Is on a sudden brought
Of a past night, and a far different scene.
Headlands stood out into the moonlit deep
As clearly as at noon;
The spring-tide's brimming flow
Heaved dazzlingly between;
Houses, with long white sweep,
Girdled the glistening bay;
Behind, through the soft air,
The blue haze-cradled mountains spread away.
That night was far more fair—
But the same restless pacings to and fro,
And the same vainly throbbing heart was there,
And the same bright, calm moon.

And the calm moonlight seems to say, —
*Hast thou, then, still the old unquiet breast,*
*Which neither deadens into rest,*
*Nor ever feels the fiery glow*
*That whirls the spirit from itself away,*
*But fluctuates to and fro,*
*Never by passion quite possessed,*
*And never quite benumbed by the world's sway?*
And I, I know not if to pray
Still to be what I am, or yield, and be
Like all the other men I see.

For most men in a brazen prison live,
Where, in the sun's hot eye,
With heads bent o'er their toil, they languidly
Their lives to some unmeaning task-work give,
Dreaming of naught beyond their prison-wall.
And as, year after year,
Fresh products of their barren labor fall
From their tired hands, and rest
Never yet comes more near,
Gloom settles slowly down over their breast.
And while they try to stem
The waves of mournful thought by which they are prest,
Death in their prison reaches them,
Unfreed, having seen nothing, still unblest.

And the rest, a few,
Escape their prison, and depart
On the wide ocean of life anew.
There the freed prisoner, where'er his heart
Listeth, will sail;
Nor doth he know how there prevail,
Despotic on that sea,
Trade-winds which cross it from eternity.
Awhile he holds some false way, undebarred
By thwarting signs, and braves
The freshening wind and blackening waves.
And then the tempest strikes him; and between
The lightning-bursts is seen
Only a driving wreck,
And the pale master on his spar-strewn deck
With anguished face and flying hair,
Grasping the rudder hard,
Still bent to make some port, he knows not where,
Still standing for some false, impossible shore.
And sterner comes the roar
Of sea and wind; and through the deepening gloom
Fainter and fainter wreck and helmsman loom,
And he too disappears, and comes no more.

Is there no life, but these alone?
Madman or slave, must man be one?

Plainness and clearness without shadow of stain!
Clearness divine!
Ye heavens, whose pure dark regions have no sign
Of languor, though so calm, and though so great
Are yet untroubled and unpassionate;
Who, though so noble, share in the world's toil,
And, though so tasked, keep free from dust and soil!
I will not say that your mild deeps retain
A tinge, it may be, of their silent pain
Who have longed deeply once, and longed in vain;
But I will rather say that you remain
A world above man's head, to let him see
How boundless might his soul's horizons be,
How vast, yet of what clear transparency!
How it were good to live there, and breathe free;
How fair a lot to fill
Is left to each man still!

MATTHEW ARNOLD

## Canopus

When quacks with pills political would dope us,
    When politics absorbs the livelong day,
I like to think about the star Canopus,
    So far, so far away.

Greatest of visioned suns, they say who list 'em;
    To weigh it science always must despair.
Its shell would hold our whole dinged solar system,
    Nor ever know 'twas there.

When temporary chairmen utter speeches,
    And frenzied henchmen howl their battle hymns,
My thoughts float out across the cosmic reaches
    To where Canopus swims.

When men are calling names and making faces,
    And all the world's ajangle and ajar,
I meditate on interstellar spaces
    And smoke a mild seegar.

For after one has had about a week of
    The arguments of friends as well as foes,
A star that has no parallax to speak of
    Conduces to repose.

B.L. TAYLOR

### Small Oratorio

Let there be pie
In the sky
When I die

In the sky
Let there be pie

There's nothing shameful in my cry!
If not for pie
What purpose in the sky?

On earth
A dearth

Whate'er his worth
That he will die
Man knows from birth

Let there be pie
Why else a sky?

D.J. ENRIGHT

### Virtue

Sweet day, so cool, so calm, so bright!
The bridal of the earth and sky—
The dew shall weep thy fall to-night;
        For thou must die.

Sweet rose, whose hue angry and brave
Bids the rash gazer wipe his eye,
Thy root is ever in its grave,
        And thou must die.

Sweet spring, full of sweet days and roses,
A box where sweets compacted lie,
My music shows ye have your closes,
        And all must die.

Only a sweet and virtuous soul,
Like seasoned timber, never gives;
But though the whole world turn to coal,
        Then chiefly lives.

GEORGE   HERBERT

### Sir Walter Ralegh's Epitaph
(*written by himself the night before his execution*)

Even such is time that takes in trust
Our youth, our joys, and all we have,
And pays us but with age and dust:
Who in the dark and silent grave
When we have wandered all our ways
Shuts up the story of our days.
And from which earth and grave and dust
The Lord shall raise me up, I trust.

SIR WALTER RALEGH

### Death

Nor dread nor hope attend
A dying animal;
A man awaits his end
Dreading and hoping all;
Many times he died,
Many times rose again.
A great man in his pride
Confronting murderous men
Casts derision upon
Supersession of breath;
He knows death to the bone—
Man has created death.

W.B. YEATS

### Lights Out

I have come to the borders of sleep,
The unfathomable deep
Forest, where all must lose
Their way, however straight
Or winding, soon or late;
They can not choose.

Many a road and track
That since the dawn's first crack
Up to the forest brink
Deceived the travellers,
Suddenly now blurs,
And in they sink.

Here love ends—
Despair, ambition ends;
All pleasure and all trouble,
Although most sweet or bitter,
Here ends, in sleep that is sweeter
Than tasks most noble.

There is not any book
Or face of dearest look
That I would not turn from now
To go into the unknown
I must enter, and leave, alone,
I know not how.

The tall forest towers:
Its cloudy foliage lowers
Ahead, shelf above shelf:
Its silence I hear and obey
That I may lose my way
And myself.

EDWARD   THOMAS

# Myth, Prophecy and Vision

The poems in this section have this in common that they extend our knowledge of reality by reference to other worlds than the ordinary one in which we live.

The aboriginal 'Lalai (Dreamtime)' provides a good example of the way folk myths enshrine sacred truths. A myth is a story or legend that embodies some truth about man or nature in a highly poetic and symbolic fashion. Although modern writers no longer believe in classical myths about the gods as the Greek and Roman poets did, they may nevertheless draw on them for inspiration and occasional allusion. And they may also create their own myths and bestow mythic stature on ordinary human figures, as Judith Wright does in her poem 'Bullocky', where the bullocky is raised to the level of an Old Testament prophet. In 'Sailing to Byzantium', Yeats transforms the civilisation that existed in Byzantium (modern Istanbul) into a symbol for a state of perfection where art and life are one. The third stanza shows how this kind of poem often develops a prophetic tone, appropriate to someone with an inspired vision of the truth.

> O sages standing in God's holy fire
> As in the gold mosaic of a wall,
> Come from the holy fire, perne in a gyre,
> And be the singing-masters of my soul.

Even if we know nothing about Yeats's view of history as a recurring circle, here suggested by the images of circular turning ('perne in a gyre'), we can respond to the inspired vision of harmony and prophetic tone.

The poem that is most obviously visionary in this section is Coleridge's 'Kubla Khan', said by the poet to have been composed in an opium dream. In it he draws on various myths concerned with true and false paradises. It is thus in some sense a poem about the poet's power to redress the Fall of Man and recapture the original paradisal state. No one has ever combined so intensely the sense of the inspired joy in poetic creation with the sense of sacred awe as Coleridge in the last lines of the poem:

> Weave a circle round him thrice,
> And close your eyes with holy dread,
> For he on honey-dew has fed,
> And drunk the milk of paradise.

With such poetry it is useless to try to paraphrase the meaning in a series of simple statements. Its whole purpose is to lift us above the mundane world of statement and argument into one of pure vision. And the same may be said of Blake's briefer visionary poem 'The Tiger'. Both poems, you will notice, employ rhythms that have an incantatory quality, similar in some respects to prophetic passages in the Bible. The voice that speaks to us in each seems a supra-human one.

All three poems by Dylan Thomas are strongly rhetorical in their rhythms, especially the bardic 'And Death Shall Have No Dominion'. Thomas was a modern Welsh poet who was a traditionalist in many respects, especially in his regard for myth, legend and symbolism. With the exception of John Donne, no poet has ever written such a triumphant and prophetic rejection of death. And his 'This Bread I Break' shows how effortlessly he weaves the sacramental images of bread and wine into his inspired verses.

Andrew Taylor in 'The Inventions of Fire' proves that it is not necessary for every poet to become an inspired bard or prophet in order to transform the sights of the ordinary world into significant myth. The voice that speaks to us in this poem is deliberately lower keyed than Coleridge's or Blake's because it knows all about the modern distrust of high flown rhetoric and rhapsodical rhythms, especially in Australia. But it has as fine a perception into magical realms as Clive Sansom, the author of 'Magic Island'. The last lines of Andrew Taylor's poem combine the wonder of a child's fairy tale with the visionary power of ancient myth and add a dash of modern incredulity.

> inside each cathedral a fish floats
> high in stone air and in a sky of glass
> he is the sun's fish dreaming of that spring
> and in his eye we swim to his dreamt heaven
> around its shores little houses are built
> and children clap at the incense of small fires.

## Lalai (Dreamtime)

*Recounted by Sam Woolagoodjah, elder of the Worora people, north-west Australia.*
*Translated by Andrew Huntley from the prose version of Michael Silverstein.*

Dreamtime,
The first ones lived, those of long ago.
They were the Wandjinas—
Like this one here, Namaaraalee.
The first ones, those days,
shifted from place to place,
In dreamtime before the floods came.
    Bird Wandjinas, crab Wandjinas
Carried the big rocks.
They threw them into the deep water
They piled them on the land.
Other Wandjinas—
all kinds—
She the rock python,
He the kangaroo,
They changed it.
They struggled with the rocks,
They dug the rivers.
These were the Wandjinas. They talk with us
at some places they have marked.
Where the sun climbs, over the hill and the river
they came,
And they are with us in the land.
We remember how they fought each other
at those places they marked—
It is dreamtime there.
Some Wandjinas went under the land,
They came to stay in the caves
And there we can see them.
Grown men listen to their Wandjinas.
    Long ago, at another time,
these Wandjinas changed the bad ones
into the rocks
And the springs we always drink from.
These places hold our spirits,
These Wunger places of the Wandjinas.

There a man learns
who his child really is:
Its spirit comes when he is dreaming
and tells him its name.
Then the man has been given his child:
It has its own name
beside the landname of its father.

Wandjina children were playing:
Plucking out his feathers
They stuck in sharp, long blades of grass
To see him use his new wings.
They did this to the first owl,
Whose name is Dunbi.

They fooled with him
They fooled with him,
They bounced him up
They bounced him up,
They tossed him up again;

But then he went over the clouds.
Namaaraalee lifted him
And he became a Wunger
For all places.

Don't take.
'Wuduu, Wuduu':
At the fire I touch you—
I hand you the strength of Wuduu,
Don't let yourself be turned.
Here on your ankle
Here on your knee
Here on your thigh,
Stay strong.
Don't let your forehead swell
(wait, wait)
Don't say the words of the men,
Don't go begging, granddaughter.

Namaaraalee is highest, he made it all,
We must keep those ways he pointed out.
Now that I have told you
We are walking to the place his body was cradled.
He is in the sky.
This half moon we will go to him.

The children who fooled with Dunbi owl
were laughing;
Then they heard the roar.
The angry Wandjinas sent a flood
And the water reached them all.

But in the wave
One man, one woman,
grabbed the tail of a kangaroo.
They clung to its tail as it swam
And it reached the rocks.
Here, on this side, they climbed up,

So that we were born,
So we go on being born.

Now you see nothing is made up,
Each father has been told what happened:
How Wandjina Namaaraalee made it all
How he sent the flood
How he said no.
Then he showed us the Wuduu that we make
for the little boys and girls:
The men who know still touch them
So each day they learn to grow.

Her two thighs, her two legs, her fingers—
The words are put there
that the Wandjinas gave us.
They said to keep on
And until today these words have lived.
The Wuduu touching will not stop,
It is our strength.
They threw spears
They killed him.
Wunumbal, Ungarinyin, were fighting
Killing each other
Living no more.

All the spirits told me then: 'Do that':
I am going back
To the place the Wandjina made for me.
All ways, do not forget,
Give away, give away.
The first one, Namaaraalee, came from the Awawarii tribe.
He had been in many fights
before he came to this land.
Here he saw the woman he wanted to keep;
But the Wandjinas all looked, then each one tugged at her.
Backward, forward—hotter and hotter—
At last they flung spears that fell like rain—
And Namaaraalee felt one drop down his side.
Then they had killed him.

These rocks are Wandjinas
Marking the fight.
When they saw he was dead
They carried him over the creek.
'Djir'—for the first one
They made that dry sound on their tongues.
Then he was laid on a fork stick cradle
High off the ground;
Now, Namaaraalee lies
in his cave on top of the rocks.

They speared him in this water,
This water is Namaaraalee.
They carried him along here,
They laid him up there.
We belong to this place,
Strangers must stay away.

I am going there now.
*We are coming to you—*
*To see you alone.*
*Are you listening?*
*That is what you wanted—*
*Namaaraalee, will you always lie down?*

*We have come to you,*
*He wanted to meet you.*
*We have always heard about you,*
*Even how you have destroyed.*

*That is what you wanted—*
*You even killed people far away.*
*You killed many people*
*When you chose to, Namaaraalee,*
*You have always done as you wanted to do.*
*And you chose to stay here:*
*You planned this as you planned your own death.*

He showed us the Wuduu we make—
He said 'Wuduu, Wuduu'.
Not just for one person—
But for all the land, all the land.
Not only for us—
Wuduu is for everyone to make.
This one is the Wandjina.

Here is a man of the Aruluuli.
He was one of them
and they brought him here—
This place belongs to him.
Those who have died are brought to the caves,
They are carried in and stay here.
A man, like this, dies at last in his cave,
His spirit is free
To leave him and wait at its Wunger place.
All his cave belongs to the Aruluuli.
        We do the same when a man dies
As the Wandjinas did for Namaaraalee
When they had killed him.
That is the way he taught us what to do,
And the way he chose to teach all other people.
He started it for everyone.

We do the same as the Wandjinas—
And Namaaraalee made this way
For all kinds of men.

At its own Wunger place
A spirit waits for birth—
'Today, I saw who the child really is—'
That is how a man
Learns to know his child.

Namaaraalee made him,
No one else,
No one.
But not all things are straight
in this day.

As I looked at the water
Of Bundaalunaa
She appeared to me:
I understood suddenly
The life in our baby—
Her name is Dragon Fly.

                    SAM   WOOLAGOODJAH

## This Bread I Break

This bread I break was once the oat,
This wine upon a foreign tree
Plunged in its fruit;
Man in the day or wind at night
Laid the crops low, broke the grape's joy.

Once in this wine the summer blood
Knocked in the flesh that decked the vine,
Once in this bread
The oat was merry in the wind;
Man broke the sun, pulled the wind down.

This flesh you break, this blood you let
Make desolation in the vein,
Were oat and grape
Born of the sensual root and sap;
My wine you drink, my bread you snap.

                    DYLAN   THOMAS

### Rediscovery

When our tears are dry on the shore
and the fishermen carry their nets home
and the seagulls return to bird island
and the laughter of children recedes at night
there shall still linger the communion we forged
the feast of oneness whose ritual we partook of
There shall still be the eternal gateman
who will close the cemetery doors
and send the late mourners away
It cannot be the music we heard that night
that still lingers in the chambers of memory
It is the new chorus of our forgotten comrades
and the halleluyahs of our second selves

KOFI   AWOONOR

### The Invention of Fire

Under every cathedral
there's a spring of pure emptiness
architects and priests search out these springs
wherever they find one a cathedral's built

without cathedrals emptiness would water the land
it would flow through the long wet lashes of grass
and under the massed white and yellow flowers
and under the faint red filmy leaves of spring
and over the sparkling stones and around the roots of trees

it would find out valleys and engrave them
with its own downward crashing capture of light
it would swell into rivers shaded and wept by willows
and join a sea forever empty of boats
forever empty of children playing on its shores
whom it aches to embrace and whose castles only
it could erase

inside each cathedral a fish floats
high in stone air and in a sky of glass
he is the sun's fish dreaming of that spring
and in his eye we swim to his dreamt heaven
around its shores little houses are built
and children clap at the incense of small fires

ANDREW   TAYLOR

## Magic Island

Travellers tell—
On yellowing, crinkled maps
Where doubtful navigation speaks
In mermaids, spouting whales,
And winds with cupid cheeks
That brought the sails
Their long-despaired-of breeze—
'There is an island, under spell,
Found at the farthest tether of our ships,
Set in enchanted seas.'


Across this isle, they say,
Fly birds of brilliant plumage, seen
In no other land: turquoise and flashing green.
And through the delicate woods strange creatures go


Fearless and free, who never know
The glint of spear or gun.
And on this island, day
Is perpetual day, the sun
Held at meridian there
Through all the Zodiac, shining
On tideless seas.


Here, in his secret cave
On couch reclining,
Lulled by the endless lap of wave
And yet informed, aware
Of every move of these
His minions, the Magician lives,
The Absolute, to whom this realm
Is subject. He gives
The sails their gusting wind; the helm
Its firm hand over reefs to the foam
Of dazzling sands;
And to these mariners
The isle's elusive spell.
Henceforth they are possessed,
Beyond the memory of all other lands,
With longing and unrest.
In time, such travellers
He turns for home,
Bemused, with tales to tell.

CLIVE SANSOM

## Kubla Khan

In Xanadu did Kubla Khan
A stately pleasure-dome decree:
Where Alph, the sacred river, ran
Through caverns measureless to man
   Down to a sunless sea.
So twice five miles of fertile ground
With walls and towers were girdled round:
And there were gardens bright with sinuous rills,
Where blossomed many an incense-bearing tree;
And here were forests ancient as the hills,
Enfolding sunny spots of greenery.

But oh! that deep romantic chasm which slanted
Down the green hill athwart a cedarn cover!
A savage place! as holy and enchanted
As e'er beneath a waning moon was haunted
By woman wailing for her demon-lover!
And from this chasm, with ceaseless turmoil seething,
As if this earth in fast thick pants were breathing,
A mighty fountain momently was forced:
Amid whose swift half-intermitted burst
Huge fragments vaulted like rebounding hail,
Or chaffy grain beneath the thresher's flail:
And 'mid these dancing rocks at once and ever
It flung up momently the sacred river.
Five miles meandering with a mazy motion
Through wood and dale the sacred river ran,
Then reached the caverns measureless to man,
And sank in tumult to a lifeless ocean:
And 'mid this tumult Kubla heard from far
Ancestral voices prophesying war!
   The shadow of the dome of pleasure
   Floated midway on the waves;
   Where was heard the mingled measure
   From the fountain and the caves.
It was a miracle of rare device,
A sunny pleasure-dome with caves of ice!

   A damsel with a dulcimer
   In a vision once I saw:
   It was an Abyssinian maid,
   And on her dulcimer she played,
   Singing of Mount Abora.
   Could I revive within me
   Her symphony and song,
   To such a deep delight 'twould win me,
That with music loud and long,
I would build that dome in air,
That sunny dome! those caves of ice!

And all who heard should see them there,
And all should cry, Beware! Beware!
His flashing eyes, his floating hair!
Weave a circle round him thrice,
And close your eyes with holy dread,
For he on honey-dew hath fed,
And drunk the milk of Paradise.

SAMUEL   TAYLOR   COLERIDGE

## The Tiger

Tiger! Tiger! burning bright
In the forests of the night,
What immortal hand or eye
Could frame thy fearful symmetry?

In what distant deeps or skies
Burnt the fire of thine eyes?
On what wings dare he aspire?
What the hand dare seize the fire?

And what shoulder, and what art,
Could twist the sinews of thy heart?
And when thy heart began to beat,
What dread hand, and what dread feet?

What the hammer? what the chain?
In what furnace was thy brain?
What the anvil? what dread grasp
Dare its deadly terrors clasp?

When the stars threw down their spears,
And watered heaven with their tears,
Did he smile his work to see?
Did he who made the Lamb make thee?

Tiger! Tiger! burning bright
In the forests of the night,
What immortal hand or eye,
Dare frame thy fearful symmetry?

WILLIAM   BLAKE

### Crow's Fall

When Crow was white he decided the sun was too white.
He decided it glared much too whitely.
He decided to attack it and defeat it.

He got his strength flush and in full glitter.
He clawed and fluffed his rage up.
He aimed his beak direct at the sun's centre.

He laughed himself to the centre of himself

And attacked.

At his battle cry trees grew suddenly old,
Shadows flattened.

But the sun brightened—
It brightened, and Crow returned charred black.

He opened his mouth but what came out was charred black.

'Up there', he managed,
'Where white is black and black is white, I won.'

TED   HUGHES

### The Black Beast

Where is the Black Beast?
Crow, like an owl, swivelled his head.
Where is the Black Beast?
Crow hid in its bed, to ambush it.
Where is the Black Beast?
Crow sat in its chair, telling loud lies against the Black Beast.
Where is it?
Crow shouted after midnight, pounding the wall with a last.
Where is the Black Beast?
Crow split his enemy's skull to the pineal gland.
Where is the Black Beast?
Crow crucified a frog under a microscope, he peered into the brain of a dogfish.
Where is the Black Beast?
Crow killed his brother and turned him inside out to stare at his colour.
Where is the Black Beast?
Crow roasted the earth to a clinker, he charged into space—
Where is the Black Beast?
The silences of space decamped, space flitted in every direction—
Where is the Black Beast?
Crow flailed immensely through the vacuum, he screeched after the
    disappearing stars—
Where is it? Where is the Black Beast?

TED   HUGHES

## And Death Shall Have No Dominion

And death shall have no dominion.
Dead men naked they shall be one
With the man in the wind and the west moon;
When their bones are picked clean and the clean bones gone,
They shall have stars at elbow and foot;
Though they go mad they shall be sane,
Though they sink through the sea they shall rise again;
Though lovers be lost love shall not;
And death shall have no dominion.

And death shall have no dominion.
Under the windings of the sea
They lying long shall not die windily;
Twisting on racks when sinews give way,
Strapped to a wheel, yet they shall not break;
Faith in their hands shall snap in two,
And the unicorn evils run them through;
Split all ends up they shan't crack;
And death shall have no dominion.

And death shall have no dominion.
No more may gulls cry at their ears
Or waves break loud on the seashores;
Where blew a flower may a flower no more
Lift its head to the blows of the rain;
Though they be mad and dead as nails,
Heads of the characters hammer through daisies;
Break in the sun till the sun breaks down,
And death shall have no dominion.

DYLAN   THOMAS

## The Hand that Signed the Paper

The hand that signed the paper felled a city;
Five sovereign fingers taxed the breath,
Doubled the globe of dead and halved a country;
These five kings did a king to death.

The mighty hand leads to a sloping shoulder,
The finger joints are cramped with chalk;
A goose's quill has put an end to murder
That put an end to talk.

The hand that signed the treaty bred a fever,
And famine grew, and locusts came;
Great is the hand that holds dominion over
Man by a scribbled name.

The five kings count the dead but do not soften
The crusted wound nor stroke the brow;
A hand rules pity as a hand rules heaven;
Hands have no tears to flow.

DYLAN  THOMAS

## South of My Days

South of my days' circle, part of my blood's country,
rises that tableland, high delicate outline
of bony slopes wincing under the winter,
low trees blue-leaved and olive, outcropping granite—
clean, lean, hungry country. The creek's leaf-silenced,
willow-choked, the slope a tangle of medlar and crab-apple
branching over and under, blotched with a green lichen;
and the old cottage lurches in for shelter.

O cold the black-frost night. The walls draw in to the warmth
and the old roof cracks its joints; the slung kettle
hisses a leak on the fire. Hardly to be believed that summer
will turn up again some day in a wave of rambler roses,
thrust its hot face in here to tell another yarn—
a story old Dan can spin into a blanket against the winter.
Seventy years of stories he clutches round his bones.
Seventy summers are hived in him like old honey.

Droving that year, Charleville to the Hunter,
nineteen-one it was, and the drought beginning;
sixty head left at the McIntyre, the mud round them
hardened like iron; and the yellow boy died
in the sulky ahead with the gear, but the horse went on,
stopped at the Sandy Camp and waited in the evening.
It was the flies we seen first, swarming like bees.
Came to the Hunter, three hundred head of a thousand—
cruel to keep them alive—and the river was dust.

Or mustering up in the Bogongs in the autumn
when the blizzards came early. Brought them down; we brought them
down, what aren't there yet. Or driving for Cobb's on the run
up from Tamworth—Thunderbolt at the top of Hungry Hill,
and I give him a wink. I wouldn't wait long, Fred,
not if I was you; the troopers are just behind,
coming for that job at the Hillgrove. He went like a luny,
him on his big black horse.

Oh, they slide and they vanish
as he shuffles the years like a pack of conjurors' cards.
True or not, it's all the same; and the frost on the roof
cracks like a whip, and the back-log breaks into ash.
Wake, old man. This is winter, and the yarns are over.
No one is listening.
            South of my days' circle
I know it dark against the stars, the high lean country
full of old stories that still go walking in my sleep.

JUDITH   WRIGHT


## Bullocky

Beside his heavy-shouldered team,
thirsty with drought and chilled with rain,
he weathered all the striding years
till they ran widdershins in his brain:

Till the long solitary tracks
etched deeper with each lurching load
were populous before his eyes,
and fiends and angels used his road.

All the long straining journey grew
a mad apocalyptic dream,
and he old Moses, and the slaves
his suffering and stubborn team.

Then in his evening camp beneath
the half-light pillars of the trees
he filled the steepled cone of night
with shouted prayers and prophecies.

While past the camp fire's crimson ring
the star-struck darkness cupped him round,
and centuries of cattlebells
rang with their sweet uneasy sound.

Grass is across the waggon-tracks,
and plough strikes bone beneath the grass,
and vineyards cover all the slopes
where the dead teams were used to pass.

O vine, grow close upon that bone
and hold it with your rooted hand.
The prophet Moses feeds the grape,
and fruitful is the Promised Land.

JUDITH   WRIGHT

## Alfred and the Phone-Boxes

Alfred wanted to use phone-boxes
for changing into someone magnificent.
He knew it was possible, because
Clark Kent could do it — sap to ZAP!
What a crowd-stopper: the sight of Super-Alf
stalking from the booth with bright cape flapping,
limbs a-ripple, gleaming like a Dulux testimonial,
and even more so
his torso!
With a mere flick of his chest
he'd speed aloft, zipping through the dazzled air —

No such luck.
Always the phone-boxes were occupied,
filling up with words and dead weight.
No room inside.
Often it was his grandfather
who'd got in there first, and was trying to grow
lettuce and silver beet, and build stone walls
taller than wide.

Once Alfred was explaining his problem to Grace,
telling her this heavy tale of booths
crammed with the rocks and vegies of his past,
when she pointed into the distance;
and as her other hand rested on his arm, he saw
a phone-box quietly levitating, up, up and away.

IAN   REID

## Delphi, Mycenae, Knossos and Elsewhere

Tourist coaches wind them up the hill, new pilgrims
to the ancient temples; stepping down, they sniff
high air above the olives, stroll
and call across the vanished courtyards, climb
on rubbled masonry, descend the trenches, teeter
on the remnant city walls, seeking
all the while a column of some little height
and solid girth to 'pose' against,
the tiny dramas of the self,
chin  in chest out and hand on hip,
the endless instamatic photos . . .
Daylong against the broken columns
and changeless sky
the pilgrims are busy with ritual
seeking perhaps to celebrate
the triumph of flesh over stone.

GEOFF   PAGE

## Sailing to Byzantium

### I

That is no country for old men. The young
In one another's arms, birds in the trees
—Those dying generations—at their song,
The salmon-falls, the mackerel-crowded seas,
Fish, flesh, or fowl commend all summer long
Whatever is begotten, born, and dies.
Caught in that sensual music all neglect
Monuments of unageing intellect.

### II

An aged man is but a paltry thing,
A tattered coat upon a stick, unless
Soul clap its hands and sing, and louder sing
For every tatter in its mortal dress,
Nor is there singing school but studying
Monuments of its own magnificence;
And therefore I have sailed the seas and come
To the holy city of Byzantium.

### III

O sages standing in God's holy fire
As in the gold mosaic of a wall,
Come from the holy fire, perne in a gyre,
And be the singing-masters of my soul.
Consume my heart away; sick with desire
And fastened to a dying animal
It knows not what it is; and gather me
Into the artifice of eternity.

### IV

Once out of nature I shall never take
My bodily form from any natural thing,
But such a form as Grecian goldsmiths make
Of hammered gold and gold enamelling
To keep a drowsy Emperor awake;
Or set upon a golden bough to sing
To lords and ladies of Byzantium
Of what is past, or passing, or to come.

W.B. YEATS

# The Poet's Eye

The poet has a deeper insight than most people into man's relationship with everything else in the universe, as Shakespeare suggests in a speech in *A Midsummer Night's Dream:*

> The poet's eye, in a fine frenzy rolling
> Doth glance from heaven to earth, from earth to heaven;
> And, as imagination bodies forth
> The forms of things unknown, the poet's pen
> Turns them to shapes, and gives to airy nothing
> A local habitation and a name.

The poems in this section show how the poet's eye sees into a great variety of relationships, those with parents and family, lovers, houses, animals, the earth, and cities. They show, too, how individual each poet's vision is, and how this individuality is expressed through the pattern of the poem itself, by the poet's choice of verse form, by the nature of the imagery, the exact quality of the language, and the tone of voice.

R.F. Brissenden, Christine Churches, Bruce Dawe, and Peter Skrzynecki all write poems about family relationships, each seeing them differently. Bruce Dawe, throughout his poem 'Condolences of the Season', creates a special language, voice and tone to suggest a relationship of secret understanding between himself and his baby son, when surrounded by the 'diddums chorus', the 'ickle-man alleluia' of adoring relatives. In 'My Mother and the Trees', Christine Churches makes us feel the mother's faith in new growth and her dominating presence, as she organises her children, 'reluctant slaves and unbelievers', into carrying water to the trees. The poet does this by combining images of authority with images from nature, such as 'From fibres of air, she wove us there/the hope of leaves', which make the mother seem one with nature's processes. The imagery of Peter Skrzynecki's two poems about family relations establish the complicated tensions that often exist in an ethnic community. While the Polish father keeps pace 'only with the Joneses/Of his own mind's making', because he is independent and totally unaffected by his new Australian environment, the Catholic mother is ambitious for her son's social and wordly success. Only a poet who had experienced these tensions at first hand could provide such a vivid insight into the patterns of relationship in migrant families.

A comparison of D.H. Lawrence's 'A Young Wife' and Geoff Page's 'Dancing Lesson' will show how different two poet's vision of love may be. Everything in Lawrence's poem suggests the dark mystery of love, while the details in Page's poem are commonplace and lightheartedly presented, as he contrasts the two dancing couples; and yet the poem embodies the important truth that love and joy are not the sole possession of young honeymoon couples but can survive into old age.

The house we live in often becomes associated in our minds with various relationships, and with our most intense hopes and fears. For McAuley the thought of his boyhood home brings back old associations from the past. He remembers with wonder his single-minded study of trains, while for Edward Thomas entry into a new house awakens fearful visions of the future. Peter Murphy's 'House on Fire' demonstrates that the poet's eye sometimes sees truths that we would prefer to keep hidden. All leads up to the isolated last line: 'We have come to see our neighbour's house burn down.'

At times we become startlingly aware of the 'otherness' of animals, the life of the earth, and the life of cities. But it is the poet who gives this awareness pattern and permanent form. The Australian poet Douglas Stewart, in his poem 'To Lie on the Grass', brings out in a natural unaffected voice and manner the contrast between the solitary figure half asleep and the busy activity of ant, spider and grasshopper, 'the little kingdoms' he refers to in the fourth stanza. The sense of the otherness of the insect or animal kingdom is doubled for the poet who visits a foreign land; as we may see from D.H. Lawrence's 'Kangaroo'. The pattern of this poem dramatises the very process by which he dissociates himself from the familiar Northern world and grapples with the antipodean strangeness represented by the kangaroo. The length of the poem and its vigorous free verse form are necessary for capturing the poet's long honest struggle with the sense of otherness and strange beauty suggested by the kangaroo. In the line, 'on the long flat skis of her legs', Lawrence describes the unfamiliar through the familiar, while elsewhere in the poem the descriptive details are sharply accurate, building up a vivid picture of the kangaroo's appearance, yet miraculously combining a sense of wonder and awe with strict objectivity.

Even though most people in Australia live in cities, many Australian poets express a strong and loving relationship with the life of the earth. This comes out most clearly in Les Murray's 'Laconics: Forty Acres', but it is also present in the poems by Thomas Shapcott, Geoffrey Dutton, and John Griffin. James McAuley, in the poem 'In the Huon Valley', implies that there is a close identity between man and the seasons when he celebrates the joys and rewards of autumn, a time of harvesting and rich fruition.

To contrast with the poems celebrating man's relationship with the earth are some poems that express man's uneasy relationship with the modern city: the most notable is Carl Sandburg's 'Chicago', which uses a vigorous free verse form to conjure up the rough brawling life of a great industrial city.

### Condolences of the Season
*To my son (born December 1964)*

And now it seems that you and I, my son,
must suffer with like fortitude
the diddums chorus, the ickle-man alleluia,
together with such other ritual oddments
as maiden aunt and grand-dam can devise . . .
                                    For months to come
your crabbed infant-elderly countenance
must be mulled over to the tea-cup's chink,
a matronly cosmogony of mums
hover above your pram or basinette
and by an infallible process of recall
place each distinctive trait (the eyes, for instance,
which could only be Uncle Tom's, nobody else's,
Aunt Lena's rugged chin, of course and, yes,
who could mistake those ears of Cousin Ted's?)

Identi-Kitted out as fulsomely
as the most Wanted criminal, any means
you choose to shake them off are bound to fail
—bearded, double-chinned, dark-spectacled,
the hair grown long and thatching tell-tale ears,
cheeks padded with the lard of middle-age
—you'll fancy the trail cold, the pack confused,
until, at a family reunion, some frail
octogenarian creature, screaming out,
'How could I be so foolish? Harry's nose!'
shaking with recognition pulls you down . . .

Lapped in a bunny-rug, you stare them out
and, smarter than they realize, play it dumb,
while, slung for burping purposes across
your mother's shoulder, all is well I see,
catching your droll heretical wink at me . . .

BRUCE  DAWE

## My Mother and the Trees

She shook the doormat free of dogs,
struck the tank to measure water, as she
marshalled us with iron buckets
to carry rations for the trees.

From fibres of air, she wove us there
the hope of leaves,
and in the flat and tepid dust
she dreamed a dwelling place of shade.

Summer by summer we carted water, slopped
lopsided up and back across the paddock:
the promised land a skeleton of stakes and hessian,
her voice insistent that they lived.

Reluctant slaves and unbelievers,
we sat out of sight
with our feet in the buckets, as she
filled the sky to the brim with trees.

CHRISTINE   CHURCHES

## Feliks Skrzynecki

My gentle father
Kept pace only with the Joneses
Of his own mind's making—
Loved his garden like an only child,
Spent years walking its perimeter
From sunrise to sleep.
Alert, brisk and silent,
He swept its paths
Ten times around the world.

Hands darkened
From cement, fingers with cracks
Like the sods he broke,
I often wondered how he existed
On five or six hours' sleep each night—
Why his arms didn't fall off
From the soil he turned
And tobacco he rolled.

His Polish friends
Always shook hands too violently,
I thought . . . *Feliks Skrzynecki*,
That formal address
I never got used to.
Talking, they reminisced
About farms where paddocks flowered
With corn and wheat,
Horses they bred, pigs
They were skilled in slaughtering.
Five years of forced labour in Germany
Did not dull the softness of his blue eyes.


I never once heard
Him complain of work, the weather
Or pain. When twice
They dug cancer out of his foot,
His comment was:'but I'm alive'.


Growing older, I
Remember words he taught me,
Remnants of a language
I inherited unknowingly—
The curse that damned
A crew-cut, grey-haired
Department clerk
Who asked me in dancing-bear grunts:
'Did your father ever attempt to learn English?'


On the back steps of his house,
Bordered by golden cypress,
Lawns—geraniums younger
Than both parents,
My father sits out the evening
With his dog, smoking,
Watching stars and street lights come on,
Happy as I have never been.


At thirteen,
Stumbling over tenses in Caesar's *Gallic War*,
I forgot my first Polish word.
He repeated it so I never forgot.
After that, like a dumb prophet,
Watched me pegging my tents
Further and further south of Hadrian's Wall.

PETER   SKRZYNECKI

## St Patrick's College

Impressed by the uniforms
Of her employer's sons,
Mother enrolled me at St Pat's
With never a thought
To fees and expenses—wanting only
'What was best'.

From the roof
Of the secondary school block
Our Lady watched
With outstretched arms,
Her face overshadowed by clouds.
Mother crossed herself
As she left me at the office—
Said a prayer
For my future intentions,
Under the principal's window
I stuck pine needles
Into the motto
On my breast:
*Luceat Lux Vesta*
I thought was a brand of soap.

For eight years
I walked Strathfield's paths and streets,
Played chasings up and down
The station's ten ramps—
Caught the 414 bus
Like a foreign tourist,
Uncertain of my destination
Every time I got off.

For eight years
I carried the blue, black and gold
I'd been privileged to wear:
Learnt my conjugations
And Christian decorums for homework,
Was never too bright at science
But good at spelling;
Could say The Lord's Prayer
In Latin, all in one breath.

My last day there
Mass was offered up
For our departing intentions,
Our Lady still watching
Above, unchanged by eight years' weather.

With closed eyes
I fervently counted
The seventy-eight pages
Of my *Venite Adoremus*,
Saw equations I never understood
Rubbed off the blackboard,
Voices at bus stops, litanies and hymns
Taking the right-hand turn
Out of Edgar Street for good;
Prayed that Mother would someday be pleased.
With what she'd got for her money—
That the darkness around me
Wasn't 'for the best'
Before I let my light shine.

PETER   SKRZYNECKI

## Building a Terrace

Sentimental nonsense of course to talk
Of the 'living rock' or the 'honesty' of stone—
But the words are in my mind each time I dig
Some stubborn chunk of sandstone out of the earth,
Split, dress and settle it into place
In wall or terrace; and I think of two dead men:
My grandfather, Will Rogers, and Archimedes.
'Give me a lever,' he said, 'and I'll shift the world.'
Rocks that a man can't lift can smash a foot—
And when, after crowbar, shovel and mattock have done
Their work, you feel a big stone gently tilt
And shift at a sweating finger's touch you know
In your bones what the old Greek meant. Archimedes
May have been just a name to Grandad, but
He loved stone and worked it till he died.
Seventy-five he was and stood as straight
As when he'd landed thirty years before
With his box of tools, his family and his lodge
Certificate: Oddfellows Master at Bridgnorth
In Shropshire—*Amicitia, amor*
*Et veritas* beneath the eye of God.
In Sydney it meant nothing. But he worked:
Anonymous flagged paths, hearths, terraces,
Fireplaces that draw and walls that stand
Are his memorial. He whistled, sang,
Was gentle, smelled of mortar, sawdust, sweat
And the open air. 'Drunk again,' he'd say,
Laughing under old-fashioned moustaches when
I fell running to watch him split the stone.

He was an artist—he could knock a tune
Out of an old tin can, they said—and when
His sledge-hammer rang on his steel wedges the rock
Broke clean and straight. I touched the fresh
Rock-faces that had never seen the sun.
At home, he said, sinking a well they found
A frog alive inside a hollow rock
Ten feet beneath the ground. He built a wall
The day before he died—surprised by death
Like that old man in Syracuse who fell
Under the ignorant Roman soldier's spear
Face down across his drawings in the sand.

R.F. BRISSENDEN

## Dancing Lesson
*a honeymoon in the Barossa*

Married a week,
high on the future
and Hardy's red,
we danced at
the Weinstube,
bodies abandoned
in a wheeling sphere
of sound, ballooned
for far horizons.

Anchored
in a corner,
a man and wife,
German perhaps—and older,
completed their meal
and watched us,
unimpressed.

Later, incredibly,
a waltz began.
They rose (with a nod)
to the floor, beginning
a slow bravura,
swoops and turns,
a long achievement of seasons;
treading together exactly
the steady high wires
of the dance.

This time
we sat it out,
still drinking—
making a balanced
descent.

GEOFF PAGE

## A Young Wife

The pain of loving you
Is almost more than I can bear.

I walk in fear of you.
The darkness starts up where
You stand, and the night comes through
Your eyes when you look at me.

Ah never before did I see
The shadows that live in the sun!

Now every tall glad tree
Turns round its back to the sun
And looks down on the ground, to see
The shadow it used to shun.

At the foot of each glowing thing
A night lies looking up.

Oh, and I want to sing
And dance, but I can't lift up
My eyes from the shadows: dark
They lie spilt round the cup.

What is it?—Hark
The faint fine seethe in the air!

Like the seething sound in a shell!
It is death still seething where
The wild-flower shakes its bell
And the skylark twinkles blue—

The pain of loving you
Is almost more than I can bear

D.H. LAWRENCE

## Their Faces Shone Under Some Radiance

Their faces shone under some radiance
Of mingled moonlight and lamplight
That turned the empty kisses into meaning,
The island of such penny love
Into a costly country, the graves
That neighboured them to wells of warmth,
(And skeletons had sap). One minute
Their faces shone; the midnight rain
Hung pointed in the wind,
Before the moon shifted and the sap ran out,
She, in her cheap frock, saying some cheap thing,
And he replying,
Not knowing radiance came and passed.
The suicides parade again, now ripe for dying.

DYLAN   THOMAS


## The Revelation

I awoke happy, the house
Was strange, voices
Were across a gap
Through which a girl
Came and paused,
Reaching out to me—

Then I remembered
What I had dreamed—
A girl
One whom I knew well
Leaned on the door of my car
And stroked my hand—

I shall pass her on the street
We shall say trivial things
To each other
But I shall never cease
To search her eyes
For that quiet look—

WILLIAM   CARLOS   WILLIAMS

## The New House

Now first, as I shut the door,
I was alone
In the new house; and the wind
Began to moan.

Old at once was the house,
And I was old;
My ears were teased with the dread
Of what was foretold,

Nights of storm, days of mist, without end;
Sad days when the sun
Shone in vain: Old griefs, and griefs
Not yet begun.

All was foretold me; naught
Could I foresee;
But I learnt how the wind would sound
After these things should be.

EDWARD THOMAS

## House on Fire

A sunset like oranges and flames like tears
and the smell of heat and charcoal and smoke
and darkness like the sea and rooms of fire

that is what has brought us here

this shrieking frame of a house we know
as it sputters and crackles and crashes and shatters
while we stand around and do not speak
and stare into the fall of night

We have come for this
to see the flames across each other's eyes
and to hear the careful boom between our ears
under control now as it peters out

We have come to see these breaking limbs and
to lower our heads before a flag of fire

We have come to see our neighbour's house burn down.

PETER  MURPHY

### Nu-Plastik Fanfare Red

I declare myself:
I am painting my room red.
Because they haven't any
flat red suitable for interiors,
because their acres of colour-card
are snowy with daylight only,
because it will look like Danger! Explosives.
or would you prefer a basement cabaret?
a decent home where Italians moved in.
Chiswick House (yes, I've gilded the mirror)
or simply infernal—


I rejoice to be doing it
with quick-drying plastic.
for small area decoration.
I tear at the wall, brush speeding:
let's expand this limited stuff!
It dries impetuously in patches,
I at edges too late scrub: this is a fight.
I accepted the conditions,
and the unbroken wall is yet to come.
Clear stretches screech into clots,
streak into smokiness.
Botched job this, my instant
hell! and no re-sale value, Dad:
a cliché too. Well, too bad.


It's satisfying to note
this mix is right for pottery.
(Good glad shock of seeing
that red-figure vases *are*.
Not 4th-edition-earthy, but stab-colour.
new-wine, red-Attis-flower, the full howl.)
My inward amphora!


Even thus shyly to surface:
up we go red, flag-balloon,
broomstick-rocket!
Brandishing blood and fire, pumping
lungs external as leaves!
Ours is a red land, sour
with blood it has not shed,
money not lost, risks evaded,
blood it has forgotten, dried
in furnace airs that vainly

figure (since wool and mines are doing well)
the fire. Torpor
of a disallowed abortion.

Why not a red room?

JUDITH   RODRIGUEZ

## Portrait of the Artist as an Old Man

In my father's house are many cobwebs.
I prefer not to live there—the ghosts
disturb me. I sleep in a loft
over the coach-house, and each morning cross
**through a rearguard of hedges to wander in the house**
It looks as though it grew out of the ground
among its oaks and pines, under the great
ark of Moreton Bay figs.
My study is the largest room unstairs;
there, on wet days, I write
archaic poems at a cedar table.
Only portraits and spiders inhabit the hall
of Courland Penders . . . however,
I check the place each day for new arrivals.
Once, in the summerhouse, I found a pair
of diamond sparrows nesting on a sofa
among warped racquets and abandoned things.
Nobody visits Courland Penders; the town
is miles downriver, and few know me there.
Once there were houses nearby. They are gone
wherever houses go when they
fall down or burn down or are taken away on lorries.
It is peaceful enough. Birdsong flutes from the trees
seeking me among memories and clocks.
When night or winter comes, I light a fire
and watch the flames
rise and fall like waves. I regret nothing.

MICHAEL   DRANSFIELD

## Numbers and Makes

The house we lived in faced the western line.
I used to sit and write the number down
Of every locomotive as it passed:
From the humdrum all-stations-into-town,

To the great thunderers that shook the house.
And passengers would wave back from the train.
I would watch out for when the signals moved
To stop or slow or all clear, and then strain

To catch the oncoming noise around the bend.
Or sometimes for variety I'd perch
Where I could note the make of every car
That passed along the street. Pure research,

Disinterested—but why, and into what?
There was no question then, no answer now.
Why change the memory into metaphors
That solitary child would disavow?

JAMES  McAULEY

## Young

A thousand doors ago
when I was a lonely kid
in a big house with four
garages and it was summer
as long as I could remember,
I lay on the lawn at night,
clover wrinkling under me,
the wise stars bedding over me,
my mother's window a funnel
of yellow heat running out,
my father's window, half shut,
an eye where sleepers pass,
and the boards of the house
were smooth and white as wax
and probably a million leaves
sailed on their strange stalks
as the crickets ticked together
and I, in my brand new body,
which was not a woman's yet,
told the stars my questions
and thought God could really see
the heat and the painted light,
elbows, knees, dreams, goodnight.

ANNE  SEXTON

## A Constable Calls

His bicycle stood at the window-sill,
The rubber cowl of a mud-splasher
Skirting the front mudguard,
Its fat black handlegrips

Heating in sunlight, the 'spud'
Of the dynamo gleaming and cocked back,
The pedal treads hanging relieved
Of the boot of the law.

His cap was upside down
On the floor, next his chair.
The line of its pressure ran like a bevel
In his slightly sweating hair.

He had unstrapped
The heavy ledger, and my father
Was making tillage returns
In acres, roods, and perches.

Arithmetic and fear.
I sat staring at the polished holster
With its buttoned flap, the braid cord
Looped into the revolver butt.

'Any other root crops?
Mangolds? Marrowstems? Anything like that?
'No.' But was there not a line
Of turnips where the seed ran out

In the potato field? I assumed
Small guilts and sat
Imagining the black hole in the barracks.
He stood up, shifted the baton-case

Further round on his belt,
Closed the domesday book,
Fitted his cap back with two hands,
And looked at me as he said goodbye.

A shadow bobbed in the window.
He was snapping the carrier spring
Over the ledger. His boot pushed off
And the bicycle ticked, ticked, ticked.

SEAMUS   HEANEY

## When I Went to the Circus

When I went to the circus that had pitched on the waste lot
it was full of uneasy people
frightened of the bare earth and the temporary canvas
and the smell of horses and other beasts
instead of merely the smell of man.

Monkeys rode rather grey and wizened
on curly plump piebald ponies
and the children uttered a little cry—
and dogs jumped through hoops and turned somersaults
and then the geese scuttled in in a little flock
and round the ring they went to the sound of the whip
then doubled, and back, with a funny up-flutter of wings—
and the children suddenly shouted out.
Then came the hush again, like a hush of fear.

The tight-rope lady, pink and blonde and nude-looking, with a few gold
    spangles
footed cautiously out on the rope, turned prettily, spun round
bowed, and lifted her foot in her hand, smiled, swung her parasol
to another balance, tripped round, poised, and slowly sank
her handsome thighs down, down, till she slept her splendid body on the rope.
When she rose, tilting her parasol, and smiled at the cautious people
they cheered, but nervously.
The trapeze man, slim and beautiful and like a fish in the air
swung great curves through the upper space, and came down
like a star
—And the people applauded, with hollow, frightened applause.

The elephants, huge and grey, loomed their curved bulk through the dusk
and sat up, taking strange postures, showing the pink soles of their feet
and curling their precious live trunks like ammonites
and moving always with soft slow precision
as when a great ship moves to anchor.
The people watched and wondered, and seemed to resent the mystery that lies
    in beasts.

Horse, gay horses, swirling round and plaiting
in a long line, their heads laid over each other's necks;
they were happy, they enjoyed it;
all the creatures seemed to enjoy the game
in the circus, with their circus people.

But the audience, compelled to wonder
compelled to admire the bright rhythms of moving bodies
compelled to see the delicate skill of flickering human bodies
flesh flamey and a little heroic, even in a tumbling clown,
they were not really happy.
There was no gushing response, as there is at the film.

When modern people see the carnal body dauntless and flickering gay
playing among the elements neatly, beyond competition
and displaying no personality,
modern people are depressed.

Modern people feel themselves at a disadvantage.
They know they have no bodies that could play among the elements.
They have only their personalities, that are best seen flat, on the film,
flat personalities in two dimensions, imponderable and touchless.

And they grudge the circus people the swooping gay weight of limbs
that flower in mere movement,
and they grudge them the immediate, physical understanding they have with
    their circus beasts,
and they grudge them their circus-life altogether.

Yet the strange, almost frightened shout of delight that comes now and then
    from the children
shows that the children vaguely know how cheated they are of their birthright
in the bright wild circus flesh.

                                                    D.H.  LAWRENCE

## Kangaroo

In the northern hemisphere
Life seems to leap at the air, or skim under the wind
Like stages on rocky ground, or pawing horses, or springy scut-tailed rabbits.

Or else rush horizontal to charge at the sky's horizon,
Like bulls or bisons or wild pigs.

Or slip like water slippery towards its ends,
As foxes, stoats, and wolves, and prairie dogs.

Only mice, and moles, and rats, and badgers, and beavers, and perhaps bears
Seem belly-plumbed to the earth's mid-navel.
Or frogs that when they leap come flop, and flop to the centre of the earth.

But the yellow antipodal Kangaroo, when she sits up,
Who can unseat her, like a liquid drop that is heavy, and just touches earth.

The downward drip.
The down-urge,
So much denser than cold-blooded frogs.

Delicate mother Kangaroo
Sitting up there rabbit-wise, but huge, plumb-weighted,
And lifting her beautiful slender face, oh! so much more gently and finely
    lined than a rabbit's, or than a hare's,
Lifting her face to nibble at a round white peppermint drop, which she loves,
    sensitive mother Kangaroo.

Her sensitive, long, pure-bred face.
Her full antipodal eyes, so dark,
So big and quiet and remote, having watched so many empty dawns in silent
    Australia.

Her little loose hands, and drooping Victorian shoulders.
And then her great weight below the waist, her vast pale belly
With a thin young yellow little paw hanging out, and straggle of a long thin
    ear, like ribbon,
Like a funny trimming to the middle of her belly, thin little dangle of an
    immature paw, and one thin ear.

'Her belly, her big haunches
And in addition, the great muscular python-stretch of her tail.

There, she shan't have any more peppermint drops.
So she wistfully, sensitively sniffs the air, and then turns, goes off in slow sad
    leaps.

On the long flat skis of her legs,
Steered and propelled by that steel-strong snake of a tail.

Stops again, half turns, inquisitive to look back.
While something stirs quickly in her belly, and a lean little face comes out, as
    from a window,
Peaked and a bit dismayed,
Only to disappear again quickly away from the sight of the world, to snuggle
    down in the warmth,
Leaving the trail of a different paw hanging out.

Still she watches with eternal, cocked wistfulness!
How full her eyes are, like the full, fathomless, shining eyes of an Australian
    black-boy.
Who has been lost so many centuries on the margins of existence!

She watches with insatiable wistfulness.
Untold centuries of watching for something to come,
For a new signal from life, in that silent lost land of the South.

Where nothing bites but insects and snakes and the sun, small life.
Where no bull roared, no cow ever lowed, no stag cried, no leopard screeched,
    no lion coughed, no dog barked,
But all was silent save for parrots occasionally, in the haunted blue bush.

Wistfully watching, with wonderful liquid eyes.
And all her weight, all her blood, dripping sack-wise down towards the earth's
    centre,
And the live little one taking in its paw at the door of her belly.

Leap then, and come down on the line that draws to the earth's deep, heavy
    centre.

                                                                D.H. LAWRENCE

## The Red Hawk

The red hawk hangs upon the wind
And the wind strips the ridges bare:
All things go with it but the mind
That rides at peace in hurrying air.

And in the silence finds its voice,
Leaving like larks its songs behind:
The tempests come, they keep their poise;
The seasons change and they are there.

Blow then, and strip these blonding plains,
These delicate round hills. The blind
Are murderous, yet the hawk remains
And all of time in his still stare.

DAVID   CAMPBELL

## Grasshopper

A grasshopper clings crazily
to a blade of grass,
almost upside-down,
leaning back.

Behind its wings
a man with a knapsack spray
steps closer.
Farther off

is the man's hut—
and more distant,
high up, blue ridges of basalt,
beyond them a city, the sea,

ships ploughing their small patches
of ocean. And beyond the sea
is land, a city, a blue
serration of basalt, a hut,

a man moving closer to a grasshopper, who,
leaning back, clings more crazily
and trembles on a blade of grass.

ROGER   McDONALD

## A Cat

She had a name among the children;
But no one loved though someone owned
Her, locked her out of doors at bedtime
And had her kittens duly drowned.

In Spring, nevertheless, this cat
Ate blackbirds, thrushes, nightingales,
And birds of bright voice and plume and flight,
As well as scraps from neighbours' pails.

I loathed and hated her for this;
One speckle on a thrush's breast
Was worth a million such; and yet
She lived long, till God gave her rest.

EDWARD   THOMAS

## To Lie on the Grass

To lie on the grass and watch,
Amused and indifferent,
The fever that drives the ant
To nowhere that matters much;

To lie on the grass with the moths
While, spry with the thought of murder,
Goes scurrying by the spider
Speckled and muttering oaths;

To lie on the grass in a dream
Where nothing will start or stir
But the grasshopper splashing the air
With a flicker of yellow flame;

Oh, to be half asleep
In the peace of the sunlit pasture
Is to lie like a lion at leisure
Where the little kingdoms creep,

And suddenly to be confused
By a prickle of spine and hair
And a notion of eyes in the air
Indifferent and amused.

DOUGLAS   STEWART

## In the Huon Valley

Propped boughs are heavy with apples,
Springtime quite forgotten.
Pears ripen yellow. The wasp
Knows where windfalls lie rotten.

Juices grow rich with sun.
These autumn days are still:
The glassy river reflects
Elm-gold up the hill,

And big white plumes of rushes.
Life is full of returns;
It isn't true that one never
Profits, never learns:

Something is gathered in,
Worth the lifting and stacking;
Apples roll through the graders,
The sheds are noisy with packing.

JAMES McAULEY

## Laconics: The Forty Acres

We have bought the Forty Acres,
prime brush land.

If Bunyah is a fillet
this paddock is the eye.

The creek half-moons it,
log-deep, or parting rocks.

The corn-ground by now
has had forty years' grassed spell.

Up in the swamp
are paperbarks, coin-sized frogs—

The Forty, at last,
our beautiful deep land

it was Jim's, it was Allan's,
it was Reg's, it is Dad's—

Brett wanted it next
but he'd evicted Dad:

for bitter porridge
many cold returns.

That interior machinegun,
my chainsaw, drops dead timber.

Where we burn the heaps
we'll plant kikuyu grass.

Ecology? Sure.
But also husbandry.

And the orchard will go there,
and we'll re-roof the bare pole barn.

Our croft, our Downs,
our sober, shining land.

LES  A.  MURRAY

## In the Forest

Wait for the axe sound in the forest.
The birds wait. The lizards pause
and wait. The creatures that are nearest
earth feel the approaching pace

measure the axeman. And they must wait.
Then has the time come? The dark
of forest is so solid that
its intergrowth should never break.

*But has the time come?* The birds
are nervous, see them flinch and turn.
The snake moves into the reeds
quickly. Danger, the signs warn.

That! Slap of an axe. That!
There, quick, over there. The tree
is tensed. In its green height
the possums clutch their young. They flee.

Crack again crack of slow man's weapon,
intolerable wait for the one tree's sake
for its grasping fall and its death to happen
and the gash in the forest, and light to break.

*Now,* says the axe, and the tree is fallen,
the spider crushed in its secret nest.
The late slow lives have been taken,
in the sheltering tree they have been crushed.

The accepted world is quickly broken,
the skull of the forest is opened up.
Now, means the axe. But the birds have forgotten
they have claimed other trees. They settle for sleep.

THOMAS   SHAPCOTT

## The Dam in February

Six feet down yet breathing air
I walk down deeper, over the tiny, dry canyons
Where once the water was like brown ice,
Down near the bottom, deeper than twice my height.

Two acres of land that should be water. No one
Since my thirteen year old son was a baby had seen it dry.
Now he rides the farmbike over and up and over.

One anxious spoonbill and two blue cranes
Share with us the last two feet of water,
And one bunyip carp that floundered down in a flood.

The yabbees are labyrinthine cool in mud,
The willows are like the dead legionnaires in *Beau Geste*
Propped on the fortress walls. There is the tyre
The children rolled down the bank ten years ago,
The blue bucket lost on a yabbeeing picnic,
Someone's brandy bottle from the catchment hills,
And under the bony willows the sick black spread
Of the tractor inner tube the children dived off.

No trace of the model yachts, thrashing gunwale-under,
No sign of the dog walking in till his ears were floating,
No feather of the eight whizzing wild ducklings,
Only casts of the feet of sheep, hieroglyphic birds,
Phantom foxes, and yabbee sticks of a year ago.

No one who lives in the cities, and lives off the country,
Could tell me the truth of this drying dam
And all those things dying that lived by it.
For a dam is a paradox, a death that's not permanent,
A statement of despair that could be cancelled by a thunderstorm,
By a sheeptrack creek tossing enormous boughs.

The country weathers out its scabby wounds.
Mud may butter up the cuts of canyons
And even the willows may yet shed their death;
They are not telling the secrets of their roots.

My son draws dust behind the motorbike,
The panting footvalve of the pump
Draws a few last gallons to the yellowing garden.

Ten years ago the drought broke. And when again?
Those who live without clocks are the true believers in time.
Only the city-dweller can afford despair,
The luxuries of pessimism, safe by the twist of a tap,
And the deep drainage taking the shit away.
How steadfast the hermit yabbee's cell of mud!

GEOFFREY   DUTTON

## Italian Lettuce

Someone's sister turned smuggler,
toe of a shoe to do the job,
after the holiday back home.

The lettuce seed was childhood
calling to her, nostalgia
from the mountain town.
Across the suburbs, brother to uncle,
to uncle's cousin, his friend,
the man from the next town,
the seeds and the seedlings spread.

It has been naturalized now,
like gnocchi, tomato paste,
pasta and pizza
and backyard wine.

If good rains come
in early summer, I expect
a bursting of leaves,
a pepper of green
all over my garden.
A week or two
and we gather a salad
on summer nights.
It's bitter and crisp
(but I'm used to it now)
and its names change
from house to house

I like that uninhibited green
that forces the light
across my stretch of yard.

JOHN   GRIFFIN

## Asphodel

Under this real estate—squared street on street
of split-level houses
with carport, garden swing—a chain
of waterlily ponds, arm of a sea
that has long since receded,
still sleeps under the still sleep of this suburb, showing itself
in flashes after rain.

We used to spend whole days there, skylarking
on an inch of blood-red water
we harried black marsh-birds through weed-thick shallows, the moon rose
heavy beneath us;
it tugged at our heels.
Now kids swing between pines, small limbs at nightfall
shine in the trees.

And once I almost drowned, stepping from clear skies ankle deep
into aeons of mud. I gaped. The earth
rushed in, my body's herds in sudden panic, then with a clamour
the night: I saw my life
of now-I-lay-me-down and milk and clean sheets out of reach
on the lily-pond's black surface
—and was dragged out by the hair.

Face down in the bladey grass and pummeled alive again I gagged
on unfamiliar breath, my belly's
mud gave up its frogspawn, lily-pods, swamp-water whelmed in cataclysms
and broke from my lungs. Having been filled
a moment with its strangeness, I discovered
a lifelong taste for earth; gills fluttered at my throat, plant fossils
creaked in my thumbs.

Now the pond too is drained. Petrol bowsers
mark the spot where twice I took my small life down to touch
the kingdom of fishbones
and came up again. Station wagons
cruise under the leaves, lawn-sprinklers turn, overhead
through bars of moon-washed cloud-wrack
the nightlights of planes.

A frog gulps on the path, earth-bubble-green. Deep water
speaks in its throat.
And revenant at dawn a pale light ghosts among wrought-iron garden chairs
          a shoal
of vanished lily-ponds. I walk
on their clear light again and will not sink
— not this time. The garden
glows. Earth holds firm under my heel.

DAVID   MALOUF

## Sydney and the Bush

When Sydney and the Bush first met
there was no open ground
and men and girls, in chains and not,
all made an urgent sound.

Then convicts bled and warders bred,
the Bush went back and back,
the men of Fire and of Earth
became White men and Black.

When Sydney ordered lavish books
and warmed her feet with coal
the Bush came skylarking to town
and gave poor folk a soul.

Then bushmen sank and factories rose
and warders set the tone—
the Bush, in quarter-acre blocks,
helped families hold their own,

When Sydney and the Bush meet now
there is antipathy
and fashionable suburbs float
at night, far out to sea.

When Sydney rules without the Bush
she is a warders' shop
with heavy dancing overhead
the music will not stop

and when the drummers want a laugh
Australians are sent up.
When Sydney and the Bush meet now
There is no common ground.

LES  A.  MURRAY

## Off the Map

All night headlamps dazzle
the leaves. Truck-drivers
throbbing on pills
climb out of the sleep

of farmtowns prim
behind moonlit lace, bronze Anzacs
dozing, leaden-headed,
at ease between wars,

and out into a dream
of apple-orchards, paddocks
tumbling with mice,
bridges that slog the air,

black piers, bright water, silos
moonstruck, pointing nowhere
like saints practising stillness
in a ripple of grain.

They thunder across country
like the daredevil boys
of the 'Fifties who flourished
a pistol in banks,

and rode off into headlines
and hills or into legends
that hang, grey-ghostly, over
campfires in the rain.

Now kids, barefooted, wade
in the warm, hatched tyre-marks
of country dust, the print
of monsters; cattle stare.

All night through the upland silence
and ranges of our skull
in low gear shifting skyward
they climb towards dawn.

A lit butt glows, a beercan
clatters. Strung out
on the hills, new streets that glow
in the eyes of farmboys, cities

alive only at nightfall
that span a continent.
Nameless, not to be found
by day on any map.

DAVID   MALOUF

## Chicago

Hog Butcher for the World,
Tool Maker, Stacker of Wheat,
Player with Railroads and the Nation's Freight Handler;
Stormy, husky, brawling,
City of the Big Shoulders:

They tell me you are wicked and I believe them, for I have seen your painted
women under the gas lamps luring the farm boys.
And they tell me you are crooked and I answer: Yes, it is true I have seen the
gunman kill and go free to kill again.
And they tell me you are brutal and my reply is: On the faces of women and
children I have seen the marks of wanton hunger.
And having answered so I turn once more to those who sneer at this my city,
and I give them back the sneer and say to them:
Come and show me another city with lifted head singing so proud to be alive
and coarse and strong and cunning.
Flinging magnetic curses amid the toil of piling job on job, here is a tall bold
slugger set vivid against the little soft cities;

Fierce as a dog with tongue lapping for action, cunning as a savage pitted
   against the wilderness,
     Bareheaded,
     Shoveling,
     Wrecking,
     Planning,
     Building, breaking, rebuilding,
Under the smoke, dust all over his mouth, laughing with white teeth,
Under the terrible burden of destiny laughing as a young man laughs,
Laughing even as an ignorant fighter laughs who has never lost a battle,
Bragging and laughing that under his wrist is the pulse, and under his ribs the
   heart of the people,
                       Laughing!
Laughing the stormy, husky, brawling laughter of Youth, half-naked,
   sweating, proud to be Hog Butcher, Tool Maker, Stacker of Wheat, Player
   with Railroads and Freight Handler to the Nation.

                               CARL  SANDBURG

# Experimental

There is always a certain amount of experimenting to find new poetic forms. Some writers try out concrete poetry in which words are arranged in shapes on the page. A simple example would be a heart shape made of repetitions of one person's name with another person's name running through it diagonally in the shape of an arrow. Or a mobile could be made out of separate words and phrases: life, love, death, evil, joy, good, is, give me, I want, I defy, etc., which would swing in the wind to give changing sentences. Concrete poetry is essentially visual rather than oral, and is often very trivial.

A much more important development is on the borderline between prose and verse. When most poetry was metrical it was possible to maintain a fairly rigid distinction between verse and prose. There was, however, one great exception, the King James Bible. Many parts of the Bible are clearly prose, though divided into verses of one or more sentences in length. Equally obviously, other parts of the Bible though written out in the same form are translations of poetry and retain the nature of poetry. The rhythms, imagery, and repetition in the psalms, for instance, mark them as poetry, though some very prosaic modern versions obscure this fact.

Nowadays poets are again exploring the boundaries of prose and verse. Galway Kinnell combines diary entries with poems, and several other poets are writing parabolas, short pieces of continuous prose rather than lineated free verse. This short section contains brief examples, together with the comments of two poets with very different views on the rejection of metre.

## To Every Thing There Is a Season

1 To every thing there is a season, and a time to every purpose under the heaven:

2 A time to be born, and a time to die; a time to plant, and a time to pluck up that which is planted;

3 A time to kill, and a time to heal; a time to break down, and a time to build up;

4 A time to weep, and a time to laugh; a time to mourn, and a time to dance;

5 A time to cast away stones, and a time to gather stones together; a time to embrace, and a time to refrain from embracing;

6 A time to seek, and a time to lose; a time to keep, and a time to cast away;

7 A time to rend, and a time to sew; a time to keep silence, and a time to speak;

8 A time to love, and a time to hate; a time for war, and a time for peace.

9 What profit hath he that worketh in that wherein he laboureth?

10 I have seen the travail which God hath given to the sons of men to be exercised therewith.

11 He hath made everything beautiful in its time: also he hath set the world in their heart, yet so that man cannot find out the work that God hath done from the beginning even to the end.

12 I know that there is nothing better for them, than to rejoice, and to do good so long as they live.

13 And also that every man should eat and drink, and enjoy good in all his labour, is the gift of God.

14 I know that, whatsoever God doeth, it shall be for ever: nothing can be put to it, nor anything taken from it: and God hath done it, that men should fear before him.

15 That which is hath been already; and that which is to be hath already been: and God seeketh again that which is passed away.

ECCLESIASTES


## Poem

'To break the pentameter, that was the first heave.'
Afterwards it wasn't so difficult.
First sentences had to go.
Next, phrases.

Now we stand looking
with some kind of
modesty, perhaps?
at the last
and trickiest
one.

Come on boys it's easy.
Come on.
it's

JUDITH WRIGHT

## Poetry

The old forms are like birdhouses that
have been made homes so long they are
full of stuffing. Only the rarest birds
can squeeze in and out of the doorways. And
then they can't move around much inside, but
keep peeping the same sounds. Which the
stuffing almost entirely insulates. But
still they stay stuck, up on their poles.
And we keep listening hard for voices
to come out of them. And they do.

GREG   KUZMA

## Middle of the Way
*for Inés*

1

I wake in the night,
An old ache in the shoulder blades.
I lie amazed under the trees
That creak a little in the dark,
The giant trees of the world.

I lie on earth the way
Flames lie in the woodpile,
Or as an imprint, in sperm, of what is to be.
I love the earth, and always
In its darknesses I am a stranger.

2

6 A.M. Water frozen again. Melted it and made tea. Ate a raw egg and the last
orange. Refreshed by a long sleep. The trail practically indistinguishable under
8" of snow. 9.30 A.M. Snow up to my knees in places. Sweat begins freezing
under my shirt when I stop to rest. The woods are filled, anyway, with the
windy noise of the first streams. 10.30 A.M. The sun at last. The snow starts to
melt off the boughs at once, falling with little ticking sounds. Mist clouds are
lying in the valleys. 11.45 A.M. Slow, glittering breakers roll in on the beaches
ten miles away, very blue and calm, as if it were Honolulu down there. Odd to
see it while sitting in snow. 12 noon. An inexplicable sense of joy, as if some
happy news had been transmitted to me directly, by-passing the brain. 2 P.M.
From the top of Gauldy I look back into Hebo valley. Castle Rock sticks into a
cloud. A cool breeze comes up from the valley, it is a fresh, earthly wind and
tastes of snow and trees. It is not like those transcendental breezes that make
the heart ache. It brings happiness. 2.30 P.M. Lost the trail. A big woodpecker
watches me wade about through the snow trying to locate it. The sun has gone

back of the trees. 3.10 P.M. Still hunting for the trail. Getting cold. From an elevation I have an open view to the SE, a world of timberless, white hills, rolling, weirdly wrinkled. Above them a pale half moon. 3.45 P.M. Going on by map and compass. I saw a deer a minute ago, he fled touching down every fifteen feet or so. 7.30 P.M. Made camp near the head of Alder Creek. Trampled a bed into the snow and filled it with boughs. Concocted a little fire in the darkness. Ate pork and beans. A slug or two of whisky burnt my throat. The night very clear. Very cold. That half moon is up there and a lot of stars have come out among the treetops. The fire has fallen to coals.

3

The coals go out,
The last smoke weaves up
Losing itself in the stars.
This is my first night to lie
In the uncreating dark.

In the heart of a man
There sleeps a green worm
That has spun the heart about itself,
And that shall dream itself black wings
One day to break free into the beautiful black sky.

I leave my eyes open,
I lie here and forget our life,
All I see is we float out
Into the emptiness, among the great stars,
On this little vessel without lights.

I know that I love the day,
The sun on the mountain, the Pacific
Shiny and accomplishing itself in breakers,
But I know I live half alive in the world,
I know half my life belongs to the wild darkness.

GALWAY   KINNELL

### Undercover Agent

Slyest of spies, our man in waiting insinuates himself into the company of prominent people at a masked garden party. Covertly sidling from group to group, he gathers vital information and takes furtive notes. His disguise is secure until, as the music starts to quicken, he becomes reckless with rhythm, pulls off all his clothes, flings data to the winds, dances wildly on his hands, laughs, cart-wheels, shouts: 'I'm giving myself away!'

IAN   REID

## Almost Indistinguishable from the World

*Almost indistinguishable from the world, we made another world which is where we live. We began very early but the job is still incomplete, which is the only point in which our world differs from the other world. The other world is complete: it consists of its past and its present. That is all there is to it. But our world builds towards its future like a plant towards fruit. Some day the fruit will appear, or some day it won't. Whichever happens is not significant. What will be—what is—significant is that our world is always incomplete, the other world always complete. And although apart from that the two worlds are identical, we can never know the other world. Never.*

ANDREW   TAYLOR

# Appendix: On Discussing Poetry

## Approaches

Students often worry unduly about having to write examination answers on poetry. It is quite natural not to want to discuss a poem as soon as you have read it, since most good poems need to be read many times, preferably aloud, before we feel at home with them. It is equally natural not to want to pick something to pieces that has just given us pleasure, something that is mysterious, strange and beautiful. But then poetic analysis is not just picking to pieces, nor necessarily destructive. It can increase our understanding and enjoyment by revealing the exact pattern of meaning the poet has created and by establishing the precise tones of voice and rhythm that give the poem its individuality.

There is no single right way of discussing poetry, no set of rules to be learned and obeyed. The best advice is to find a poem you like, a poem that seems to have something special to say to you. Read it over and over aloud until it has become a part of you and you know some or all of it by heart and then gradually try to explain to yourself why you like it. You will soon find that you are thinking not only about *what* the poem says but *how* it says it. And that is the essence of all poetic analysis and poetic appreciation: the recognition of the close relationship between meaning and form, content and pattern.

In order to describe this relationship and communicate what you have discovered to others, it is necessary to know one or two things about the main poetic kinds (song, sonnet, elegy, etc.) and the various forms of versification (blank verse, heroic couplets, rhymed stanzas, free verse). A word of caution is needed here. In writing about a poem, it is pointless to carry out a detailed analysis of its vowel sounds or its rhyme scheme or any other aspect of the poet's technique unless you relate your observations to the meaning of the words and the pattern of the poem as a whole. Some of the worst discussions and examination answers are crammed with irrelevant and mechanical remarks about sound and rhythm. Equally bad are answers full of gushing emotion unrelated to the words and shape of the poem. Remember always that meaning and form are inseparable.

## Versification

A poet chooses a particular verse form because it seems appropriate to the rhythm and pattern of his experience and because earlier poets have already given proof of its appropriateness. Even poets who decide to alter or ignore former models are nevertheless conscious that they belong to a great and long tradition. And all readers appreciate a pleasing blend of the familiar and the new.

For most practical purposes, versification can be divided into two main systems. These are *metrical verse* and *free verse*.

METRICAL VERSE

This is verse in which there is a regular alternation of stressed and unstressed syllables. The basic metrical unit is the *foot,* which is like the bar in music. The commonest type of line in English poetry has five feet, as in the opening line of Keats's sonnet:

When I | have fears | that I | may cease | to be

where x marks an unstressed syllable and / marks a stressed syllable. Most handbooks, using terms taken from Latin versification, describe this type of line as an *iambic pentameter:* an *iamb* is a foot consisting of an unstressed syllable followed by a stressed (may cease), *pentameter* means that there are five feet in the line. This basic pattern occurs in the blank verse of Shakespeare's plays, the heroic couplet, the sonnet, and many other forms.

For many poets, especially those who write poems to be set to music, the unit is the flowing musical phrase. Moreover, meaning, grammatical structure, alternation of single syllable and multi-syllabled words, punctuation, pitch, and pace all affect the music of verse.

To describe the metre or music of verse you need signs. Older handbooks use two based on Latin practice. However, the use of three signs gives us a more flexible system of notation. To the signs already given for a stressed syllable (/) and an unstressed (x) we need to add one for the syllable that receives only a subordinate stress (\). Using this more flexible system we can indicate that the word 'in' in this line from Shakespeare's sonnet 'Shall I compare thee to a summer's day' receives only a subordinate stress (\) and not a normal stress (/):

When in | etern | al lines | to time | thou | grow'st.

It is often through such variations of the basic metrical pattern that poets create their best musical effects.

In metrical verse there are many ways in which lines may be grouped; into paragraphs in *blank verse*, into pairs of lines linked by rhyme in *couplets*, as in Swift's 'Satirical Elegy on the Death of a Famous General':

> Come hither, all ye empty things,
> Ye bubbles raised by breath of Kings;

and also into many different types of *stanzas* in lyric verse. A *stanza* is a form created by grouping lines together in a regular pattern, for example in Shelley's lyric 'To Night', where the seven-lined rhymed stanza, with shorter second and seventh lines, is repeated throughout the poem.

> Swiftly walk o'er the western wave,
>   Spirit of Night!
> Out of the misty eastern cave,
> Where, all the long and lone daylight,
> Thou wovest dreams of joy and fear,
> Which make thee terrible and dear, —
>   Swift be thy flight!

In stanzaic verse the same rhyme scheme is normally repeated throughout the poem; the scheme is usually described by giving each new rhyme sound a letter of the alphabet: in Shelley's poem, ababccb.

FREE VERSE

This should not be confused with blank verse, which employs regular metre but is unrhymed, as in Hamlet's speech

> To be, or not to be—that is the question.
> Whether 'tis nobler in the mind to suffer
> The slings and arrows of outrageous fortune,
> Or to take arms against a sea of troubles,
> And by opposing end them?

Free verse. as its name implies, does not use regular metrical patterns. It is rhythmic, but its rhythms are irregular and flexible, as may be seen in D.H. Lawrence's poem 'Kangaroo':

> Delicate mother Kangaroo
> Sitting up there rabbit-wise, but huge, plumb-weighted,
> And lifting her beautiful slender face, oh! so much more gently
>     and finely lined than a rabbit's, or a hare's,

The writer of free verse still uses line division and other groupings and typographical devices to ensure that we read his words as he wishes us to read them, with the right emphasis and intended rhythms.

A high proportion of the poems in this anthology are written in some form of free verse. During the last hundred years there has been a revolution in versification, with some poets like Yeats saying that they could not write without the discipline and aid of metre and other poets claiming that metrical verse was a tyranny that killed originality and free expression. Several poets in this volume actually comment on the break with traditional verse patterns. Judith Wright, in 'Poem', re-echoes the American poet Ezra Pound's sentiments:

> 'To break the pentameter, that was the first heave.'
> Afterwards it wasn't so difficult.

Then, as a traditionalist herself, she goes on ironically to invite her fellow modern poets to get rid of everything else as well. The American poet Greg Kuzma begins his poem 'Poetry' with the lines:

> The old forms are like birdhouses that
> have been made homes so long they are
> full of stuffing.

The break with traditional metres and regular rhymes has produced much great and original poetry, but it is worth recalling T.S. Eliot's remark that no verse is free. We should not make the mistake of thinking that free verse is easier to write than traditional metrical verse. On the contrary it is perhaps more difficult, since the pattern and order which are necessary in all art have to be invented afresh by the individual poet for each poem.

Where writers of metrical verse often play off the natural rhythms of speech against the artificial metrical patterns, the poet who chooses free verse goes one stage further and makes speech rhythms determine the musical pattern. But he could only do this as long as both he and his readers were familiar with the more regular rhythms of traditional English verse.

## Diction

To achieve compression of meaning and complexity of thought and emotion, the poet makes a highly selective use of the language. This choice we call *diction*. Naturally we should expect Shakespeare's diction to be very different from D.H. Lawrence's, since the language has changed greatly since the sixteenth century, and we should expect poets from different countries to use national idioms of speech; but often two poets writing in the same country and at the same time use a very different selection of words. It is revealing to compare and contrast the diction of Bruce Dawe and Judith Wright, both twentieth-century Australian poets. Judith Wright employs highly emotive language, rich in sense impressions, drawn in the main from rural life. By contrast, Bruce Dawe's diction is witty and intellectual, full of topical references to modern urban living and contemporary political issues; which is no doubt one of the reasons why he is so popular a poet in Australia today. A poet's diction is always related to his subject, to his unique vision of life, and to the practice of other poets. He creates his world through words, so it's with words that we must be concerned when we discuss poetry.

## Tone and Voice

It is not only *diction* that establishes the individual vision in a poem, but *tone* and *voice*.

The poet expresses his feelings towards his subject and his readers by a quality we can call *tone*. In ordinary life we recognise when a speaker's mood changes to one of anger or sorrow by alterations in his tone of voice as well as by what he actually says. It is the same in poetry. Some of the most subtle meanings are conveyed through slight shifts in tone or by irony and understatement. (Irony is where we imply meanings that are not directly stated.) To respond appropriately to one of Auden's poems we need to notice how the tender loving tone of the opening line is modified by the ironic tone of the second:

> Lay your sleeping head, my love
> Human on my faithless arm;

In Blake's poem 'Holy Thursday', it is important that we recognise from the start the prevailing tone of righteous indignation in the series of rhetorical questions:

> Is this a holy thing to see
> In a rich and fruitful land,
> Babes reduced to misery,
> Fed with cold and usurous hand?

Otherwise we shall not feel the full power of his social criticism.

Equally important in our response to a poem is recognition of the type of *voice* employed by the poet. To begin with, we can distinguish between the *impersonal voice* and the *personal voice*. It is fairly easy to distinguish between the impersonal voice used by Shirley in the opening lines of 'Death the Leveller':

> The glories of our blood and state
> Are shadows, not substantial things;

and the personal tone of McAuley's 'Revenant', which begins,

> I enter the familiar house
> In which I worked and ate and slept
> But twenty silent months ago.

But the distinction is not always so clear.

Since each main *kind* or *genre* of poetry has its appropriate voice, it is important that we should be able to recognise the voice so that we will know what kind of poem it is, and therefore what kind of response is expected. This is not as difficult as it sounds, for the more we read the better we become in knowing how to respond. To help readers to understand and enjoy some of the main kinds of poetry, the poems in this anthology have to some extent been grouped according to kind.

Thus in the group 'Song' you will soon come to recognise the *lyric* (singing) *voice,* and in other sections the *ballad voice,* the *elegiac voice,* the *dramatic voice,* and the *prophetic voice.* To fail to recognise the prevailing voice in poetry is rather like expecting an opera singer to sing blues or a rock singer to sing grand opera. So we need to get the voice right.

**Imagery**
One of the most obvious differences between the poet's handling of language and the prose writer's lies in the poet's handling of *imagery*. An image expresses or implies a relationship between one thing and another. Its main appeal is to the senses (not necessarily to the eye only, although *visual imagery* and *pictorial imagery* are the most common types). The poet's main concern is often with the emotions associated with the image. The most easily recognised forms of imagery are the *simile* (plural *similes*), where one thing is formally stated to be like another, and the *metaphor* where the likeness is implied not stated. Byron begins his lyric praise of his lady's beauty with a formal simile 'She walks in beauty, like the night', while in Shelley's 'Ode to the West Wind' the wind is a sustained metaphor for the creative and prophetic powers of poetry.

Images need not be either similes or metaphors, but these are the easiest to recognise. It is a great mistake to think that images are merely decorative, introduced to give a bit of extra beauty to the poem or to draw attention to the poet's powers of fine writing. Images serve a great variety of functions and you will begin to enjoy a poem more once you understand what each image is doing, how it is connected with other images, and what it contributes to the meaning of the whole.

# Acknowledgements

The editors and publishers are grateful to the following for permission to reproduce copyright material.

University of Queensland Press for 'Aboriginal Query' from **People are Legends** by Kevin Gilbert; 'The Ice Fishermen, Lake Erie' from **Ice Fishing**, 'The Nocturne in the Corner Phonebox' from **The Cool Change** and 'The Invention of Fire' from **The Invention of Fire** by Andrew Taylor; 'Suburb with Television' from **A Soapbox Omnibus** by Rodney Hall; 'Tree in the City', 'Near the School for Handicapped Children', 'The Trees: A Convict Monologue', and 'In the Forest' from **Selected Poems** by Thomas Shapcott; 'Elegy for Don McLaughlin', 'Feliks Skrzynecki', and 'St Patrick's College' from **Immigrant Chronicle** by Peter Skrzynecki; 'The Tomb of St John Learmonth, A.I.F.' from **Collected Verse** by John Manifold; 'Like This for Years', 'Pas de Deux for Lovers', and 'Portrait of the Artist as an Old Man' from **Streets of the Long Voyage** by Michael Dransfield; 'Centipede' and 'Nu-plastik Fanfare Red' from **Nu-plastik Fanfare Red** by Judith Rodriguez; 'Delphi, Mycenae, Knossos and Elsewhere', and 'Dancing Lesson' from **Smalltown Memorials** by Geoff Page; and 'Grasshopper' from **Airship** by Roger McDonald. Angus & Robertson Publishers for 'Melbourne' from **Selected Poems** by Chris Wallace-Crabbe; 'Fire Sermon', 'The Man Beneath the Tree', 'South of My Days', 'Bullocky', and 'Poem' from **Collected Poems** by Judith Wright; 'Country Places' and 'Meditation on a Bone' from **Collected Poems** by A. D. Hope; 'The Traveller' from **Selected Poems** by C. J. Dennis; 'How Gilbert Died' from **Collected Verse** by A. B. Paterson; 'The Convict and the Lady', 'Pieta', 'To Any Poet', 'Numbers and Makes', and 'In the Huon Valley' from **Collected Poems** by James McAuley; 'The Commercial Hotel', 'Noonday Axeman', 'Laconics: The Forty Acres', and 'Sydney and the Bush' from **The Vernacular Republic** by Les A. Murray; 'Suburban Sonnet' and 'Barn Owl' from **Selected Poems** by Gwen Harwood; 'Three Weeks Ago' and 'My Mother and the Trees' from **My Mother and the Trees** by Christine Churches; 'Beach Burial' from **Selected Poems** by Kenneth Slessor; 'Autobiography' from **Selected Poems** by Rosemary Dobson; and 'To Lie on the Grass' from **Selected Poems** by Douglas Stewart. David Higham Associates Limited for 'Farewell to New Zealand' by Wynford Vaughan-Thomas from **The New Oxford Book of Light Verse**; 'Fern Hill', 'Do Not Go Gentle into That Good Night', 'This Bread I Break', 'And Death Shall Have No Dominion', 'The Hand that Signed the Paper', and 'Their Faces Shone Under Some Radiance', from **Collected Poems** by Dylan Thomas published by J. M. Dent. Longman Cheshire Pty Ltd for 'The Not-So-Good Earth' from **An Eye for a Tooth**, 'Migrants' from **Beyond the Subdivisions,** 'Elegy for Drowned Children' and 'Condolences of the Season' from **A Need for a Similar Name** by Bruce Dawe. Faber and Faber Limited for 'Epitaph on a Tyrant', 'Epitaph for the Unknown Soldier', 'Lay Your Sleeping Head', 'If I Could Tell You', and 'The Secret Agent' from **Collected Poems** by W. H. Auden; 'The Sunlight on the Garden' from **Collected Poems** by Louis MacNiece; 'Money' from **Complete Poems** by Randall Jarrell; 'Journey of the Magi' from **Collected Poems 1909-1962** by T. S. Eliot; 'Crow's Fall' and 'The Black Beast' from **Crow** by Ted Hughes; and 'A Constable Calls' by Seamus Heaney. Bolt & Watson Ltd for 'The Sensitive Philanthropist' and 'An Ew Erra' from **Daughters of Earth**, and 'Small Oratorio' from **Sad Ires** by D. J. Enright, published by Chatto & Windus Ltd. Oxford University Press for 'Always a Suspect' from **Sounds of a Cowhide Drum** by Oswald Mbuyiseni (1972), and 'A Consumer's Report' from **The Last of England** by Peter Porter (1970). Andrew Taylor for 'How to Spend New Year's Eve Alone'. Michael and Anne Yeats and Macmillan London Limited for 'The Ballad of Moll Magee', 'The Wild Swans at Coole', 'Death', and 'Sailing to Byzantium', from **Collected Poems** by W. B. Yeats. South Head Press for 'Fairy Stories' and 'The Words Are There' from **I Learn by Doing** by Craig Powell; 'Europe' from **Poetry Australia** 1977 by John Tranter; 'Lalai' (Dreamtime) from **Poetry Australia** 1976 by Sam Woolagoodjah; and 'House on Fire' from **Poetry Australia** 1974 by Peter Murphy. Chatto & Windus Ltd for 'Missing Dates' from **Collected Poems** by William Empson. Nicholas Hasluck for 'Test Cricket'. Ian Reid for 'The Coat', 'Beached', 'Alfred and the Phone-Boxes', and 'Undercover Agent' from **Undercover Agent** published by Adelaide University Union Press. Martin Secker & Warburg Limited for 'The Choice' from **The Early Drowned** by Hilary Corke. John Murray (Publishers) Ltd for 'In Westminster Abbey' and 'Executive' from **Collected Poems** by John Betjeman. McLelland and Stewart Limited for 'Meeting of Strangers' from **The Collected Poems of Earle Birney** by Earle Birney. John Griffin for 'Cross-Reference' and 'Italian Lettuce' published by Adelaide University Union Press. Geoffrey Dutton for 'The Island Day' and 'The Dam in February'. Heinemann Educational Books Ltd for 'Rediscovery' by Kofi Awoonor from **A Book of African Verse** (Reed and Wake). Australian National University Press for 'Building a Terrace' from **Building a Terrace** by R. F. Brissenden. New Directions Publishing Corporation for 'The Revelation' from **Collected Earlier Poems** by William Carlos Williams © 1938. Harcourt Brace Jovanovich, Inc., for 'Chicago' from **Chicago Poems** by Carl Sandburg © 1916 by Holt, Reinhart and Winston, Inc., © 1944 by Carl Sandburg.

Cover:  William Blake (1757-1827) English
       Illustrations to Dante's Divine Comedy Inferno, Canto VII
       The Stygian Lake
       Pen and watercolour over pencil
       52.4 x 36.8 cm
       Inscribed l.r. Hell Canto 7
       Felton Bequest 1920

       Reproduced by permission of the National Gallery of Victoria, Melbourne

Cover design by Julie Gross

# Glossary of Poetic Terms

**allegory** in its simplest and most obvious form is a story that carries a moral significance; the best example is *Pilgrim's Progress,* in which Christian journeys to the Celestial City. But there need not be a story. Allegory is the presentation of one thing by something else (verb *allegorise,* adj. *allegoric*).

**alliteration** the repetition of similar sounds, particularly initial sounds, e.g. 'O Wild West Wind' (adj. *alliterative*).

**antithesis** a figure of speech in which two different ideas are expressed in balanced contrast, e.g. 'A cherub's face, a reptile all the rest' (adj. *antithetic*).

**ballad stanza** a four-lined stanza, with four stresses in the first and third lines and three stresses in the second and fourth, which normally rhyme. Australian ballads often employ a longer stanza with lengthier lines.

**blank verse** unrhymed ten-syllable lines, traditionally described as unrhymed iambic pentameters.

**couplet** two successive lines linked together by end-rhyme. The commonest types are the ten-syllable couplets (*heroic couplets*) much favoured by such eighteenth-century poets as Pope, and eight-syllable (*octosyllabic*) couplets as used by Swift. Where the sense is complete at the end of a couplet it is called *end-stopped,* where the sense flows on into the following lines it is *run-on.*

**elegy** a poem expressing grief; more generally any poem of a subjective or meditative nature.

**epigram** a brief witty poem, often of only two lines, that makes its point by extreme conciseness of expression, e.g. Rochester's 'Impromptu on Charles II'.

**epitaph** a brief poem in memory of someone who is dead, brief because originally intended to be placed on a tombstone over the grave.

**free verse** a form of verse that comes close to the natural rhythms of speech and normally does not use regular metrical patterns or rhymes; for further details see the 'Preface' and 'On Discussing Poetry'.

**image** a word or phrase that appeals to the sense and suggests a relationship between two or more things or facets of experience; the main appeal may be to any one or more of the five senses (sight, sound, touch, smell or taste) or to the intellect as in Donne's witty metaphysical imagery.

**irony** a word of very wide meaning in discussions of poetry. At its simplest, irony is to say one thing and intend another; it involves a contrast between what is stated and what is implied — wryly, wittily, sardonically, or in some other way. Through irony a poet often defines or establishes his attitude towards his subject and his reader. Compare *tone.*

**lyric** originally poetry that was intended to be sung to the lyre; it has come to mean poetry that expresses personal emotions, poetry that is song-like and poetry composed to be set to music.

**ode** in ancient literature, a poem adapted to be sung, originally by the chorus in a Greek play; in modern use, a rhymed (rarely unrhymed) lyric, often in the form of a formal address to a person or personified power, generally dignified or exalted in subject, feeling and style, but sometimes simple and familiar, although less so than in song.

**onomatopoeia** the use of words whose sounds help to suggest the meaning. But notice that sounds alone, separated from word meaning, convey almost nothing. In discussing the sound as an echo to the sense this should be borne in mind (adj. *onomatopoeic*).

**personification** the representation of inanimate objects or abstract ideas in human terms, e.g. Keats's personification of the Greek urn as 'foster-child of silence and slow time'.

**quatrain** a stanza of four lines normally rhyming

**rhyme** a repetition of similar sounds in the final syllables of lines of verse; this is known as *end-rhyme* to distinguish it from *internal rhyme* often found in ballads.

**sonnet** a fourteen-lined lyrical poem that conforms to a set rhyme scheme (except in some modern examples). The two main schemes are (1) *Italian* (or *Petrarchan*) in which the first eight lines (*octave*) express the general theme and the last six (*sestet*) present a conclusion, the rhyme scheme being abbaabbacdecde; (2) *Shakespearean* in which the division is usually into three quatrains and a concluding couplet, thus abab cdcd efef gg.

**stanza** a fixed pattern of lines grouped together, frequently involving a rhyme scheme (adj. *stanzaic.*)

**symbolism** a presentation of the invisible world of spiritual realities and values through descriptions of the real world. Unlike *allegory,* symbolism treats the real world as a *part* of this higher reality, not simply as a means of representing it. There are two main kinds of symbols: *natural* and *private*. Examples of natural symbols are the sun in Thomas's 'This Bread I Break' and the dew in King's 'Sic Vita'. These draw on our shared knowledge and experience of the world. A private symbol achieves its special meaning through an individual poet's usage, for example Yeats sees the swans in 'The Wild Swans at Coole' as symbols of youth, strength, and love (verb *symbolise*).

**tone** a not easily defined but certainly an indispensable term to describe the poet's attitude to his subject and his reader as it is implied through choice of word, irony, rhythmic stress and other devices. Some restrict its use to the attitude to the reader.

**vers libre** an alternative term for *free verse* (French).

# Biographical Index of Poets

**Arnold, Matthew** (1822—88)   Born in Surrey, England, he was the son of a famous headmaster of Rugby school and became Professor of Poetry at Oxford.

**Auden, W.H.** (1907—73)   Born in England, he was a prominent left-wing poet in the 1930s. He lived in America for many years and later became Professor of Poetry at Oxford.

**Awooner, Kufi** (1935—   )   Born in the Volta region of Ghana, he studied at Achimota and the University of Ghana, Accra, and is well known as both a poet and a novelist.

**Bentley, Edmund Clerihew** (1875—1956)   Born in London, he was a journalist and novelist who gave his name to the verse form known as the clerihew.

**Betjeman, John** (1906—   )Educated at Marlborough and Oxford University, he is famous for his light verse and writings on Victorian art, and was made Poet Laureate in 1972.

**Birney, Earle** (1904—   )   Born in Calgary, Alberta, and educated at the Universities of British Columbia, Toronto, California and London, he is one of Canada's best known poets.

**Blake, William** (1757—1827)   Born in London and apprenticed as an engraver, he illustrated his own and others' poetry.

**Blight, John** (1913—   )   Born in South Australia, he now lives and works in Queensland.

**Brissenden, R. F.** (1928—   )   Born in Wentworthville, New South Wales, he is Reader in English at the Australian National University and Chairman of the Australian Literature Board.

**Brooke, Rupert** (1887—1915)   Educated at Rugby school and Cambridge, he expressed the early idealistic phase of World War I before his death at Scyros in the Mediterranean.

**Browning, Robert** (1812—89)   Born in London and educated at home, he married the poet Elizabeth Barrett and lived in Italy much of his life.

**Butler, Samuel** (1835—1902)   Educated at Shrewsbury School and Cambridge University, he is best known for his satiric fiction.

**Byron, George Gordon** (1788—1824)   He was one of the best known English Romantic poets and wrote satires, lyrics and narrative verse.

**Campbell, David** (1915—79)   Born in New South Wales, he played football for England and was decorated for bravery in World War I.

**Carroll, Lewis** (1832—98)   Educated at Oxford University, he became a mathematical lecturer, but is best known for writing *Alice's Adventures in Wonderland*.

**Churches, Christine** (1945—   )   She grew up in Keith, South Australia and is now married to an Anglican priest.

**Clough, Arthur Hugh** (1819—61)   Educated at Oxford University, he is remembered for his lyrics and inventive longer poems.

**Coleridge, Samuel Taylor** (1772—1834)   Born in Devon, he was educated at Christ's Hospital School and Cambridge University and achieved fame as a poet and critic.

**Corke, Hilary** (1921—   )   He published a volume of verse in 1961 and is represented in various anthologies.

**Cummings, E.E.** (1894—1962)   Born in Cambridge, Mass., he was a poet, novelist and painter and was also an early experimenter with typographical forms.

**Cunningham Allan** (1784—1842)   Born in Scotland, his fame rests mainly on his imitation of ancient ballads.

**Dawe, Bruce** (1930—   )   Born in Geelong, he worked as a farm-hand, copy-boy and postman, joined the R.A.A.F. and now lectures for a living.

**Dennis, C.J.** (1876—1962)   Born in Auburn, South Australia and educated at Christian Brothers' College, Adelaide, he became a journalist in Melbourne and is best known for *The Sentimental Bloke*.

**Dobson, Rosemary** (1920—   )   Born in Sydney, the grand-daughter of the English poet, Austin Dobson, she was educated at Sydney University, studied art, and has worked for publishing firms in England and Australia.

**Donne, John** (1572—1631)   Born in England and educated as a Catholic before he joined the Church of England, he wrote most of his love poetry before he became Dean of St Pauls in 1631.

**Dransfield, Michael** (1948—73)   Born in Sydney, he was one of the new generation of poets and wrote about the drug culture.

**Drayton, Michael** (1563—1613)   An Elizabethan poet, he is chiefly remembered for his sonnets and narrative verse.

**Dutton, Geoffrey** (1922—   )   Born in South Australia and educated at the Universities of Adelaide and Oxford, he has lectured in English, travelled widely, and is now a publisher.

**Eliot, T.S.** (1888—1964)   Born in America, he lived in England from 1915 and as a leading poet and critic greatly influenced the modern movement.

**Empson, William** (1906—   )   Born in Yorkshire, educated at Cambridge University, he was Professor of English at the Universities of Tokyo, Pekin and Sheffield, and is famous as a critic as well as a poet.

**Enright, D.J.** (1920—   )   Born in England and educated at Cambridge University, he was Professor of English at Singapore and is now a publisher.

**Fitzgerald, Edward** (1809—83)   Educated at Cambridge, his chief work was his very free verse translation of the Persian poet, Omar Khayyam.

**Ford, Thomas** (d. 1648)   A composer and musician, he published instrumental music and songs.

**Gay, John** (1685—1732)   Born in Devon, he was an eighteenth-century wit and author of the famous *Beggar's Opera.*

**Gilbert, Kevin** (1933—   )   Born at Condobolin, New South Wales, he began writing in prison and is now dedicated to the Australian aboriginal cause.

**Gilbert, W.S.** (1836—1911)   A witty writer of light verse, he is chiefly remembered for the operas he wrote with Sir Arthur Sullivan.

**Gray, Thomas** (1716—71)   A Cambridge classical scholar, his fame rests mainly on his *Elegy* and numerous Odes.

**Griffin, John** (1935—   )   Grew up in Hammond, South Australia, teaches in Adelaide and is poetry editor of the Adelaide *Advertiser.*

**Hall, Rodney** (1935—   )   Born in England, he came to Australia in 1949, was educated in Brisbane, has published several volumes of verse and is a script writer for radio and TV.

**Hardy, Thomas** (1840—1928)   Born in Dorset and trained as an architect, he achieved fame as a poet and novelist.

**Harwood, Gwen** (1920—   )   Born in Brisbane, she now lives in Tasmania and has written an opera as well as poetry.

**Hasluck, Nicholas** (1942—   )   Born in Canberra, educated at Oxford University, he is a lawyer who lives in Perth and has published fiction as well as poetry.

**Heaney, Seamus** (1939—   )   Born in Northern Ireland, he has won several awards for his poetry.

**Herbert, George** (1593—1633)   Born in England and educated at Cambridge University, he entered the Church and wrote religious verse modelled on John Donne's.

**Herrick, Robert** (1591—1674)   Educated at Cambridge University, he became a clergyman and wrote poetry about the country.

**Hood, Thomas** (1799—1845)   An English poet and wit, he is chiefly remembered for his punning verse.

**Hope, A.D.** (1907—   )   Born in New South Wales and educated at the Universities of Sydney and Oxford, he was Professor of English at the Australian National University in Canberra.

**Hopkins, Gerard Manley** (1844—89)   Born in London and converted to Catholicism at Oxford, his highly original poetry remained unpublished for thirty years after his death.

**Hughes, Ted** (1930—   )   Born in Yorkshire and educated at Cambridge University, his fame rests partly on his very original animal poems.

**Jarrell, Randall** (1914—65)   Born in America, he served in the Army Air Force and received the National Book Award for Poetry in 1961.

**Johnson, Samuel** (1709—84)   Born at Lichfield and educated at Oxford University, he was the greatest literary figure of the eighteenth century.

**Jones, Evan** (1927—   )   Born and educated in Jamaica where his father was a banana planter, he has lived and worked in England and America as a teacher and script-writer for TV and films.

**Jonson, Ben** (1572—1637)   Born and educated in London, he was a poet and dramatist whose work reflects his love of classical literature.

**Keats, John** (1795—1821)   Born in London, he studied medicine, published his first volume of poetry in 1817, and died in Rome.

**King, Henry** (1592—1669)   A poet who became Bishop of Chichester, he was a friend of John Donne and Ben Jonson.

**Kuzma, Greg** (1944—   )   Born in Rome, New York, educated at Syracuse University, he teaches English at the University of Nebraska.

**Lawrence, D.H.** (1885—1930)   Born in the English Midlands, the son of a miner, he trained as a teacher but then travelled widely and wrote highly original novels, short stories and poems.

**Lawson, Henry** (1867—1922)   Born in New South Wales of Scandinavian ancestry, he wrote short stories and poems and is Australia's best known writer.

**Lear, Edward** (1812—88)   An artist, traveller, wit and poet, he is chiefly remembered for his nonsense songs.

**McAuley, James** (1917—76)   Born in New South Wales and educated at Sydney University. He was Professor of English at the University of Tasmania, editor of *Quadrant* and a well known poet and critic.

**McCrea, John** (1872—1918)   Born in Canada, he was a distinguished doctor before serving in World War I, at first as a gunner and later in the medical corps.

**McDonald, Roger** (1941—   )   Born in Young, New South Wales, he works as an editor for the Queensland University Press, where he has helped to publish much recent Australian verse.

**Macneice, Louis** (1907—63)   Born in Belfast and educated at Oxford University, he lectured in Classics, worked for the BBC and was closely connected with the left-wing poets of the 1930s.

**Malouf, David** (1934—   )   Born in Melbourne, he graduated from Queensland University and lectured there and at Sydney. He has travelled widely and written successful fiction as well as poetry.

**Manifold, John** (1915—   )   Born in Melbourne, educated at Geelong Grammar and Cambridge University, he is a musician as well as a poet and linguist.

**Milton, John** (1608—74)   Born in London and educated at Cambridge, he visited Italy in his youth, served the Puritan side in the Civil War, and devoted his whole life to literature and the cause of freedom.

**Morant, Harry** (1865—1902)   Known as 'The Breaker', he is equally famous for his horsemanship and for his Australian ballads.

**Mtshali, Oswald Mbuyiseni** (1940—   )   Born at Vryheid, Natal, he writes with controlled anger and compassion about life in South Africa and is widely read there.

**Murphy, Peter** (1945—   )   An Australian poet who has spent most of his life in the same suburb, he writes of the strangeness behind everyday experience.

**Murray, Les A.** (1938—   )   Born in New South Wales, he was educated at country schools and Sydney University and has published numerous books of verse.

**Nashe, Thomas** (1567—1610)   A contemporary of Shakespeare, he wrote religious pamphlets, prose satire and poetry.

**Omar Khayyam** (c. 1050—c. 1123)   An astronomer-poet of Persia, he was born a tent-maker's son and enjoyed court patronage.

**Owen, Wilfred** (1893—1918)   Born in Shropshire and educated at the University of London, he enlisted in 1915, wrote poetry in hospital while recovering from war wounds, returned to the front and was killed.

**Page, Geoff** (1940—   )   Born in New South Wales, he is a school teacher and poetry reviewer to the *Canberra Times*.

**Paterson, Andrew Barton** (1864—1941)   Born in New South Wales, Banjo Paterson was educated at Sydney Grammar School, was a solicitor, war-correspondent, journalist and grazier and is best known for his ballads.

**Porter, Peter** (1929—   )   Comes from Brisbane but has lived in London since 1951, working in an advertising agency.

**Powell, Craig** (1940—   )   A graduate in medicine from Sydney University, he has contributed to many poetry magazines.

**Quarles, Francis** (1592—1644)   He was a prolific writer of prose and verse, but many of his works were destroyed as a punishment for his support of the Royalist cause in the Civil Wars.

**Ralegh, Walter** (1552—1618)   A famous Elizabethan courtier, navigator, and author, he was executed in the Tower of London in the reign of James I.

**Raleigh, Walter** (1861—1922)   A critic and poet, he was Professor of English Literature at Oxford University.

**Ransom, John Crowe** (1888—1974)   Born in Tennessee, he influenced the development of a group of Southern writers and founded the *Kenyon Review* in 1939.

**Reid, Ian** (1943—   )   Born in New Zealand, he has taught in the University of Adelaide and is now a Professor at Deakin University.

**Rochester, John Wilmot** (1648—80)   The second Earl of Rochester was a favourite of Charles II who frequently banished him from court for his satires and scandalous behaviour, but always recalled him.

**Rodriguez, Judith** (1936—   )   Born in Perth, she teaches English at La Trobe University.

**Sandburg, Carl** (1878—1967)   Born in Illinois, he worked at a variety of jobs and identified himself with the common speech and folk traditions in his poetry.

**Sansom, Clive** (1910—   )   Born in England, he has published poems and plays for adults and children and now lives in Hobart.

**Sergeant, Howard** (1914—   )   Born in Yorkshire, he qualified as an accountant and has produced anthologies of Commonwealth poetry and edited an important poetry magazine, *Outposts*.

**Sexton, Anne** (1928—74)   Born in Newton, Massachusetts, she worked as a fashion model and published several volumes of poetry.

**Shakespeare, William** (1564—1616)   Born in Stratford-on-Avon, he wrote poems in addition to plays and his sonnets were published in 1609 although many had been written much earlier.

**Shapcott, Thomas** (1935—   )   Born in Queensland, he left school at fifteen, became an accountant and has written an opera as well as many books of verse.

**Shelley, Percy Bysshe** (1792—1822)   Born in Sussex and educated at Oxford University, from where he was sent down, he left England in 1814 and spent most of the remainder of his life in Italy.

**Shirley, James** (1596—1666)   A poet and schoolmaster, he fought for the Royalists in the Civil War and was one of the last dramatists to write before the theatres were closed.

**Slessor, Kenneth** (1901—71)   Born in New South Wales, he was journalist, war correspondent and author of many poems.

**Skrzynecki, Peter** (1945—   )   He came to Australia at the age of four with his Polish Ukrainian parents and now teaches in New South Wales.

**Soyinka, Wole** (1935—   )   Born in Nigeria, he studied at University College, Ibadan, and Leeds University, and is now one of the best known African poets and playwrights.

**Stewart, Douglas** (1913—   )   Born in New Zealand, he came to Australia in 1938 and has worked for the Sydney *Bulletin* and written many verse plays and poems.

**Swift, Jonathan** (1667—1745)   One of the most famous satirists in prose and verse, he is best known for his *Gulliver's Travels*.

**Taylor, Andrew** (1940—   )   Born at Warrnambool, Victoria, and educated in Melbourne, he has travelled extensively and now lectures at the University of Adelaide.

**Taylor, B.L.** (1866—1921)   Born in England, he was the author of many amusing poems.

**Tennyson, Alfred** (1809—92)   Born in Lincolnshire and educated at Cambridge, Lord Tennyson became Poet Laureate in 1850.

**Thomas, Dylan** (1914—53)   Born in Swansea, Wales, he became famous as a BBC broadcaster before travelling to America where he died.

**Thomas, Edward** (1878—1917)   Born in London, he struggled to make a living as a writer before being killed in World War I.

**Tranter, John** (1943—   )   A Sydney-based poet, he has published several volumes of verse.

**Twain, Mark** (1835—1910)   ·An American writer, he is best known for his two masterpieces *Tom Sawyer* and *Huckleberry Finn*.

**Vaughan-Thomas, Wynford** (1908—   )   Born and educated in Wales and at Oxford University, he joined the BBC in 1937, won fame as a war correspondent, and returned to the BBC after the war.

**Wallace-Crabbe, Chris** (1934—   )   Born in Melbourne, he was educated at Scotch College and the University of Melbourne where he now teaches English.

**Watts, Alaric A.** (1797—1864)   Born in London, he was a journalist who published two volumes of poetry but is chiefly remembered for the one poem printed here.

**Wilde, Oscar** (1854—1900)   Born in Ireland, he was a poet, dramatist and famous wit.

**Williams, William Carlos** (1883—1963)   Born in New Jersey and educated in New York and Europe, he combined a profession in medicine with a literary career and was awarded a National Book Award in 1950.

**Woddis, Roger** (1917—   )   Born in England, he is a regular contributor of comic and satiric verse to the *New Statesman*.

**Woolagoodjah, Sam** (   )   He is an elder of the Worora people of north-west Australia.

**Wordsworth, William** (1770—1850)   Born in the English Lake District, he collaborated with Coleridge in producing the *Lyrical Ballads,* a volume that changed the subject matter and style of English poetry.

**Wright, Judith** (1915—   )   Born in Armidale and educated at Sydney University, she is a distinguished critic as well as a poet and an active conservationist.

**Wyatt, Thomas** (1503—42)   Born in Kent, he was a courtier and poet who wrote graceful songs and helped to introduce the sonnet to England.

**Yeats, W.B.** (1865—1939)   Born in Dublin, he studied art but adopted literature as a profession and became the leading figure in the revival of Irish literature and the modernist movement.

# Index of First Lines